The Gift of Maybe

THE
Gift
of
Maybe

Finding Hope and Possibility
in Uncertain Times

ALLISON CARMEN

A TarcherPerigee Book

tarcherperigee

an imprint of Penguin RandomHouse LLC
penguinrandomhouse.com

Copyright © 2014 by Allison Carmen
Penguin Random House supports copyright. Copyright fuels creativity, encourages diverse voices,
promotes free speech, and creates a vibrant culture. Thank you for buying an authorized
edition of this book and for complying with copyright laws by not reproducing, scanning,
or distributing any part of it in any form without permission. You are supporting writers
and allowing Penguin Random House to continue to publish books for every reader.

TarcherPerigee with tp colophon is a registered trademark of Penguin Random House LLC

Most TarcherPerigee books are available at special quantity discounts for bulk purchases
for sales promotions, premiums, fund-raising, or educational use. Special books, or book excerpts,
can also be created to fit specific needs. For details, write: Special.Markets@penguinrandomhouse.com

LIBRARY OF CONGRESS CATALOGING-IN-PUBLICATION DATA has been applied for.

ISBN 9780399169533 (trade paperback)
ISBN 9780698156036 (ebook)

PRINTED IN THE UNITED STATES OF AMERICA

Text design by Kristin del Rosario

While the author has made every effort to provide accurate telephone numbers, Internet addresses, and
other contact information at the time of publication, neither the publisher nor the author assumes any
responsibility for errors, or for changes that occur after publication. Further, the publisher does not
have any control over and does not assume any responsibility for author or third-party websites or
their content.

Dedicated to my parents,
whose love and devotion sustained me
on my journey to Maybe

CONTENTS

Introduction

. . . . .

The future ain't what it used to be.

—YOGI BERRA

For most of my life, I had an addiction that no doctor could cure. This addiction caused me anxiety, depression, sleeplessness, and sometimes such hopelessness that my next breath itself seemed a burden. My addiction wasn't to alcohol or drugs. I wasn't a shopaholic or a compulsive gambler. Yet this addiction almost destroyed me, and it afflicts millions of people around the world.

My addiction was to certainty. At every moment in my life, I desperately sought to know what was going to happen next. My need for certainty caused me to believe that the unexpected was always negative. I became devastated whenever things took an unexpected turn because I believed it meant the life I had envisioned for myself was no longer possible. I continually sacrificed my goals and desires in an effort to feel safe and secure. Yet no matter what I did I could not escape uncertainty, and the choices I made in an effort to attain certainty always led to compromise and disappointment.

The symptoms of addiction to certainty are peculiar and particular to each person, but the common denominator is unnecessary suffering. In my case, I would lie awake at night in fear of what might be, unable to catch my breath and unable to control my mind's chatter. Was my livelihood secure? Would my husband always love me? Could I afford my life? Were the stocks I invested in safe? Would my parents, children, and other family members stay well? Would there be a large-scale disaster in my city? Would I or would I not get a raise this quarter? What would the results of my annual checkup be? This onslaught of sleeplessness and anxiety began taking a toll on my immune system and I actually started getting sick.

The need to know the future had gripped me as a teenager, and most of my twenties were spent in stress. In my thirties, though I was at the top of my career as an attorney, I was deeply unhappy and suffering physically. No doctor could identify my illness, but my symptoms included an array of infections, allergies, anxiety, and depression. So I turned to alternative medicine, meditation, acupuncture, and any other practice I thought might relieve my physical and emotional pain. I found some tools to ease my mind, but when a big issue or conflict infiltrated my life, I still spun out of control. I even went so far as to become best friends with a woman with psychic abilities in hopes she could lift the veil of uncertainty and tell me what the future had in store for me.

One day, still in the midst of pressing anxiety about the future, I went to see my Qigong teacher for a lesson. I related to him my tale of woe, and he responded with a simple story that, for me, changed everything.

Here is the story.

One day, a farmer's horse ran away. His neighbor came by and said, "You have the worst luck." The farmer replied to the neighbor, "Maybe." The next day, the horse returned with five mares, and the neighbor came by and said, "You have the best luck." The farmer replied, "Maybe." The day after that, the farmer's son was riding the horse and fell off and broke his leg, and the neighbor came by and said to the farmer, "You have the worst luck." The farmer replied, "Maybe." The next day, the army came looking to draft the boy for combat but he could not go because his leg was broken. The neighbor came by and said, "You have the best luck." Again the farmer said, "Maybe."

I will remember the moment I heard this simple story for the rest of my life. It was in this moment that I was able to feel space in my breath. It was in this moment that, for the first time, I had a place to park my thoughts and just sit in a place called Maybe. In this place, it felt all right not to know the future, and suddenly I was filled with an inexplicable hope.

As time passed, I learned that this world of Maybe created hope because it allowed me to see the infinite ways that every situation *could* unfold. I realized that things might not always go as planned, but that in the next moment things would change and Maybe for the better. I had been so busy in my life worrying that the horse could run away that it never occurred to me that he could also come back.

Over time I have come to realize that Maybe is a place, a philosophy, a seed, and a magic elixir all at once. Maybe is the part of uncertainty where endless possibilities live and breathe. Maybe is not a matter of probability, as in "There is an 80 percent chance a situation could be bad and a 20 percent chance it could work out well." Instead, it is a space within the uncertainty of life, a mind-set that suggests that for every situation we experience, there are numerous ways it may resolve. Within these many possibilities, maybe there is a chance a situation that I am facing will work out well, or maybe the answer will come to me, or maybe I will be all right no matter what happens. The essence of "Maybe" or "what may be" contains the hope within uncertainty.

Some people might disagree with my interpretation of the farmer story, but I cannot deny the life-changing experience I had when I heard it for the first time. For me, Maybe became a window through which to view all that can be. Within that open space exists so many wonderful possibilities that give me hope and strength to endure uncertainty. As I began to live in the realm of Maybe, my fears of the unknown dissolved, and I established a new future filled with opportunities, a future that has me realizing many of the hopes and dreams I thought I'd sacrificed to worry long ago.

Maybe allowed me to successfully venture into a business I love, a lifelong dream. Maybe transformed many other aspects of my life, too, from my health to my relationships with the people I love. In short, Maybe changed—and saved—my life.

Today, as a life coach and business consultant, I work with

a vast array of people, from entrepreneurs and owners of multimillion-dollar companies to artists, actors, writers, fashion designers, attorneys, medical workers, parents, and the homeless. I have witnessed people who, regardless of present circumstances, found the courage to step into the realm of Maybe to improve their lives. A nanny goes back to school and becomes a nurse. A costume designer lands her first blockbuster film. A garage attendant finds more joy in everyday living. An investment banker quits his Wall Street job to pursue his passion at a private company. A screenwriter has some of the biggest names in Hollywood perform in her play. A fitness trainer makes a great living selling his photographs. An unemployed marketing executive starts her own catering business. A little boy who made a devastating, game-losing shot becomes the most valuable player on his team for the season. A divorced mother of two creates a wonderful new life for herself and her kids. A woman on the verge of business bankruptcy turns her business into a multimillion-dollar international company. An attorney finds less stress at work and wins more cases. A grandmother cares for her grandson and successfully grows her cake business at the same time. And the list goes on and on.

The results that my clients and I achieved when we

changed our perceptions of the various challenges that confronted us sometimes amaze even me. Whoever we are, whenever we embrace Maybe and move beyond what we thought was possible, we open ourselves to more success and happiness in our lives.

The possibilities are endless. I now have tens of thousands of international followers who are embracing the mind-set of Maybe through my blog, interviews, and YouTube videos. Given the fast-paced, changing economic and political landscape around the world, Maybe has become a constant for many and a refuge of hope. In writing this book, it's my hope that Maybe will transform and improve your life and help you find comfort in the unknown.

How Can Maybe Help You?

You may be wondering how something as easy as thinking or saying the word *Maybe* can have the kind of impact I am describing. That is precisely the beauty of Maybe. The idea of Maybe is so easy to apply, and at the same time it can have a profound effect on whatever part of your life you choose to apply it to. Whether you have been recently laid off from your job or you are having health concerns or money problems, whether you are looking for love or success or just looking to live life with less emotional pain, the philosophy of Maybe provides you with a tool to help you find your way. It helps you alleviate stress or worry, helps you embrace the uncertainty in your life as an opportunity, helps you enjoy the present, and helps you live with less emotional suffering. It is a mind-set that can influence all aspects of your life, a strategy you can use when life throws you an unexpected curveball. As you experience the mind-set of Maybe, it will take on a meaning unique to you. Maybe creates a space where so much more is possible. Maybe becomes the constant that never lets you down.

Maybe is not a plan or a story; it is the offer of an unfolding experience. Embracing Maybe is a process, one that evolves and will continue to improve your life in new and exciting ways. For this reason, the true power and nuance of Maybe will come to you outside the pages of this book, when you experience your first moment of joy and vigor in the face of uncertainty.

Maybe is just one change of perspective, but it is one that can change the very direction of your life. So, let's take a journey together into the land of Maybe, and may we all find a life of peace, happiness, hope, and success. Just Maybe!

ONE

The Philosophy of Maybe

. . . . .

The philosophy of Maybe simply states that for every situation we face there are numerous possibilities of resolution, and within those possibilities exists a hope that "it could be good," "it could get better," or we could find a way to accept the situation we are facing and still be all right.

Humans have an amazing ability to forget that one of the few things in life we can count on is change. The minute things take an unexpected turn, we tend to get bogged down in uncertainty. I've seen friends, family, and clients get derailed by everything from a surprise expense to an unexpected and unwelcome diagnosis. But once we begin to apply the idea of Maybe, we see that the cycle of change is never-

Every outcome offers more possibilities that lie ahead.

ending. Every outcome offers more possibilities that lie ahead.

Imagine how much stress and emotional pain we could avoid by just saying "Maybe" to any unexpected and uncertain situation in our lives—a health issue, a company merger, a rift with an old friend. We cannot know for certain how the situation in front of us will resolve. Even when it does resolve, we cannot know if it is indeed a final outcome. What seems difficult and unexpected at one moment can lead to something truly amazing in the next. As we learn to stay in Maybe, we become less reactive and stressed about whatever confronts us. Maybe allows us to transform our pain and fear of an uncertain future into hope and peace in the moment.

The reason the mind-set of Maybe is so effective and empowering is that it continuously offers us more than the one possibility that is causing us stress and keeping us up at night. We all have a choice. We can sit in the uncertainty with stress, anxiety, or total despair. Or we can realize that there *may be* a way out of the situation, a way forward, or another way for us to exist in what is before us. Before our fears materialize into certainty, Maybe offers countless possibilities.

And even if the outcome we most fear does become a reality, as it sometimes does, the next moment gives us the chance for something new once again. Within Maybe exists an eternal beacon

Before our fears materialize into certainty, Maybe offers countless possibilities.

that always lights our way. Instead of being afraid of the dark, we can stay focused on the glimmering light that gives us hope and guides us to a realm of new possibilities.

Going for Gold

When we recognize the Maybe in everything, we understand that no matter what a situation looks like in this moment, things will definitely change. Maybe can kick us into something better than we imagined.

Take this example: U.S. Olympian Michael Phelps was on a quest to win eight gold medals in the 2008 Olympics. But the autumn before the Beijing games, Phelps fell and sustained a micro fracture in his wrist. His coach is reported to have said at the time that this was the most upset he had ever seen Phelps. Michael was devastated about his wrist and kept saying, "It's over! I'm finished!" Despite the uncertainty his injury created, Michael Phelps got right back into the pool a few weeks after surgery. But he was confined to kicking in the pool with a kickboard as his teammates swam.

All that kicking, though, strengthened his legs. This was evident from the record fast turns he made in all of his races. At the finish of the one hundred meter butterfly race, his strong kick propelled his hands to the wall first by one hundredth of a second. Now Michael Phelps is the first person to ever win eight gold medals in a single Olympics, more than anyone else in Olympic history.

What if Phelps had stayed out of the pool until his hand healed and believed his dreams were finished? What Phelps perceived as a bad circumstance ended up being the foundation for him to become one of the greatest Olympians in history. Michael Phelps was quoted at the 2008 Olympics as saying, "If you dream as big as you can dream, anything is possible."

Into the Unknown

> Faith means living with uncertainty—feeling your
> way through life, letting your heart guide you like a
> lantern in the dark.
>
> **—DAN MILLMAN**

So how does this addiction to certainty start, and where can getting over it take us in our lives? It begins simply—with one fearful thought about the future. We want to know if we will keep our job, have enough money to pay for our children's college education, or meet the person of our dreams. The "not knowing" becomes the source of all of our fears and, we come to believe, the cause of all of our problems. Often a friend or family member will say to us, "Don't worry, have some faith that it will all work out." There are some who can adhere to this advice because they have cultivated faith through religious beliefs or are inherently comfortable with experiencing the uncertainty of life. But those of us who struggle with the unknown cling to our fear of "what will be." It becomes impossible to let go of how we see a particular situation and move forward in our lives without judging the future. As much as many of us would like to have faith, it is a road that can be difficult to travel.

The good news is that when we are gripped by our fears of the unknown, Maybe can help us. Maybe is a connector to lead us away from our fearful thoughts and toward an open field of hope and possibility. Maybe provides us comfort. Maybe enables us to challenge our fearful thoughts with alternatives: Maybe our thoughts are not true; Maybe something else will happen; Maybe this is good; Maybe things can get better; Maybe everything is okay. These alternatives assist us in opening our hearts to allow us to experience space and light in the midst of a crisis. Maybe creates a type of faith that helps us get through an unexpected situation with less stress and greater ease.

Finding Faith

One of my clients, Joe, lost his job as a marketing consultant. The minute he got the news, he started to panic that all of his savings would be depleted and he wouldn't be able to support his young family. For two weeks he suffered through sleepless nights, worrying that he'd be unemployed for a long time. He became very anxious. It just so happened that on day fourteen Joe got a short-term consulting job, and he started to work while still looking for long-term employment. Every week he'd say the consulting job was ending—and yet it kept getting extended. Joe was so focused on when the short-term job would end that he never stopped to consider that he was working and actually making a little more money than he had before. Over and over, he swore the job was ending on Friday, and sure enough it got extended again for another month. Whenever this happened, Joe told himself the story that imminent doom had only been postponed for a short time.

When he came to me, Joe said his wife told him to have a little more faith that things would all work out. She told him that faith was the answer to all of his worries, yet the unknown future scared Joe no matter what she said. Joe clung to his belief that since he couldn't know what tomorrow would bring, he couldn't feel safe and secure.

Joe and I started to use Maybe to question his absolute beliefs about the future. Joe began to admit that Maybe things would work out, Maybe he would get a new job, Maybe he would keep the current job, and Maybe everything was okay for now and he would figure out the rest in time. As Joe realized that there were infinite possibilities ahead even though he couldn't see them yet, he was able to relax at times and stay open to whatever life had to offer in his future. After a few sessions, I gave Joe some Maybe exercises, and we agreed to meet again in a few months.

After those few months, I met with Joe again and he was still working at the "temporary" job and was making more money this year than last. His wife was pregnant, and he was thinking about buying a new home. The idea of Maybe had helped him question his "doom and gloom" thoughts about the future and offered him other possibilities. He felt less stressed and worried about the future and was even getting comfortable with his "temporary" status at the company. "Do you think I'm developing . . . faith?" he asked me. I smiled and answered, "Maybe!"

An Invitation to Set Sail

> Your living is determined not so much by what life
> brings to you as by the attitude you bring to life,
> not so much by what happens to you as by the way
> your mind looks at what happens.
>
> **—KHALIL GIBRAN**

As we examine our belief system through the lens of Maybe, we start to see that our fear of the future is merely a creation of our own minds. It is a perception that we conjure about our reality, one fueled by an inner dialogue centered on our negativity about the future. Fears that our endeavors will result in misfortune, that we will never be able to accomplish our goals, or that we will be unable to find a way out of our predicaments lose some hold on us. In times of fear and worry, we remember to ask ourselves one simple question:

"Do we know for sure that the things we fear will work out as negatively as we are projecting?" Most often, the answer to this simple question is a resounding no. We immediately recognize that, if our fears are neither definitive nor absolute, something else must exist within our experience of uncertainty. We become aware that the space in uncertainty that is not filled by our fears falls within the realm of Maybe. And just like that, we've made room for hope and possibility.

So as we embrace Maybe to alleviate stress and worry, we start to create more opportunities, because, instead of approaching life with fear, we approach it with a sense of all that is possible. Maybe becomes our new internal dialogue, creating a vast and hopeful space within us. As we embrace it, we start to yearn less for certainty and more for our dreams, passions, and joys. The unknown becomes an invitation for us to set sail on a new adventure, to create a life that reflects who we truly are and what we want to achieve.

With Maybe we can rejoice in the fact that things are always changing. As everything remains open, there is room for our lives to grow and improve.

The Blank Piece of Paper

Laura came to me a few years into running her own architecture firm, which she had started at the young age of twenty-seven. She sought me out when she felt that she could no longer handle the stress and worry of not being able to create high-quality projects for her clients. After Laura signed a client, she would typically sit totally petrified in front of a large piece of drawing paper with a pencil in her hand. She would sit like this for hours.

Laura was scared that she had no idea what she would create for her clients, that they would not like what she created, and that she could not complete the plans in time for her deadline. Agonizing in this way, Laura faced the empty page day after day as bits and dribbles of ideas came to her. She lay awake at night thinking about what would happen if she did not come up with a good design. Would she lose her business? Could she pay the rent? Eventually Laura produced satisfactory work, but the process of getting there was excruciating.

After I shared with her the idea of Maybe, Laura was doubtful of its merit. She didn't see how it might help her. I explained that her fear and worry came from a belief that the way any given project would turn out was negative, when in fact the result was merely uncertain. "The essence of Maybe," I told her, "is that it allows us to see the uncertainty with hope, as a place for us to create something that has never been created before, a place for us

Laura was used to seeing "not knowing" as wholly negative when in fact it could be the beginning of something new and wonderful.

to tap all that is possible without being limited by the past or our fears." Laura was used to seeing "not knowing" as wholly negative when in fact it could be the beginning of something new and wonderful.

For the first time, Laura looked at me with something resembling hope on her face. She said that she had always viewed uncertainty as the enemy. To my delight, she said the thought of partnering with uncertainty made her feel free, even childlike. As we parted, Laura thanked me and said that a new project she was working on, which just a few hours before had felt heavy and burdensome, suddenly had her excited, much to her surprise.

Today Laura reports that she still begins new projects by staring at the blank piece of paper. But now she is filled with hope that within the unknown lies her creative potential.

Laura says she realizes that with a blank piece of paper in front of her she sees more possibilities for the project than she does down the road when set plans are developed and firm decisions made. Laura has alleviated so much pain and suffering with this simple shift in perspective. She feels that she is now more creative than ever, and so much more open to all the possibilities a blank page offers.

TRY THIS

· · · · ·

MAYBE IT'S OKAY

If we think about it, we can all identify a situation in our lives where we made ourselves sick with worry only to find out that everything is just fine now, if not better. These experiences help us understand Maybe.

Find a quiet moment to think about a time when you were feeling stressed and anxious about the way a situation would turn out, but in the end everything worked out in your favor. Perhaps, like me, you spent months worrying about a work review only to be told you were getting a promotion. Perhaps you were devastated when the man or woman you liked chose someone else, only to find that six months later you met the person of your dreams. Perhaps you were stressed because you lost your job, but it forced you to look at different opportunities, and now for the first time you enjoy what you are doing for a living.

Now think about a current situation, one that is causing you stress and worry. Write down a statement about how you feel about it. Are your worries and stressful thoughts absolute? Can you know for sure how things will turn out? If you are not certain, try to acknowledge that other possibilities may exist. How does this shift make you feel?

Next, challenge your statement with the idea of Maybe. Write down the following:

Maybe my beliefs about this situation are not true;
Maybe what is happening is good;
Maybe what's happening can get better;
Maybe I can find a way to accept whatever I'm experiencing and still be all right;
Maybe, in time, I will know what to do next;
Maybe everything is fine.

You can phrase these Maybe statements in your own words or use only the ones that feel right. How does your situation seem now? Do you feel more hopeful? Do you see the possibility that your fears might not come true?

Try to review these statements a few times each day. If you can, add more Maybe statements that challenge your stress and worry about the current situation. Keep your attention on these Maybe statements over the next few days and see what happens to your fears and worries.

Maybe you'll be pleasantly surprised.

TWO

Keep Hope Alive

. . . . .

Knowledge is knowing that we cannot know.
—RALPH WALDO EMERSON

Maybe is more than just an effective tool for shifting our relationship with uncertainty; it can also be the glue that holds together a positive outlook.

How many times has someone said to you, "Just stay positive and have an open mind" when you are upset or stressed about a given situation? Although it often sounds like the right attitude to adopt, trying to replace every negative thought with a positive thought can be an overwhelming task.

Our fears of uncertainty are often more powerful than our ability to be positive thinkers. Many of us can control our negative thoughts to a point, and then, when something unexpected or sharply negative happens, we lose hold of the positive thoughts. The fear of not knowing how a situation will unfold and the worry that it will not work out become all-consuming. As hard as some of us try, in times of great challenge and change we can't win the battle of positive thinking versus negative thinking.

The philosophy of Maybe is so powerful because it doesn't ask us to battle our negative thinking. Instead, Maybe dilutes the power negative thinking has over us by inviting us to see other ways a situation can work out. If a negative thought, or a fear, is not a fact that will surely happen, then what are some other possibilities? When we acknowledge that there is more than one way that a situation can unfold, and that some of these ways may just be positive, negative thoughts can no longer control us.

The idea of Maybe allows us to keep a positive and hopeful vision of our lives, and at the same time frees us from defining each and every moment as either good or bad. It is simply too painful to hold on to every event we do not like in our lives, seeing them as tragic and finite. What a joy to realize that the unexpected does not have to define our experience, but instead opens up opportunities to find new ways to accomplish our goals.

Harold and Lorna

My clients Harold and Lorna were excited about their retirement when they began the process of selling their house in New York and moving to North Carolina. Lorna told me on several occasions that she felt so positive about the move and that they had found the perfect retirement community, one that would give them the opportunity to enjoy the rest of their lives. When the contract of sale was sent out to the prospective buyers for their New York home, Lorna and Harold flew down to North Carolina and put a deposit on a new house in the retirement community. On the day they were due to return from North Carolina, I received a call from the buyer's attorney.

"Sorry," she said, "the buyers are no longer interested in the house."

The deal was dead, and I called my clients immediately to let them know. They were in the car on the way to the airport to return to New York. On hearing the news, Lorna became devastated and started to scream and cry. She lamented the fact that nothing in her life was working out lately, and this loss of the deal was just another thing to add to her pile of unhappiness. She felt that her dream of retiring to the beautiful new community no longer existed and she would lose her deposit on her new home if she could not sell the old house quickly. She told me that she was going to ask for their deposit on the new home back before the three-day option to cancel expired. For Lorna this presented a huge problem because it was one of the last homes available in the newly built retirement community.

I tried to explain to her and Harold that just because this deal had collapsed, it did not mean that they would not sell their house in time to close on their new home in North Carolina. I asked them to stay in the field of Maybe until they got back to New York and we could speak. I told Lorna that Maybe the deal would come back, Maybe another deal would come through, or Maybe it would work out in another way that we just couldn't see right then. I asked Lorna to stay positive about her dream to move to North Carolina and let Maybe dilute her negative thoughts about things not working out as planned. Lorna took a deep breath and agreed to contemplate Maybe on her ride back to New York. Harold was quiet for most of the exchange, but I could hear him at the end of the conversation say softly in the background, "That's right. Maybe."

Later that same day, the realtor from the broken deal called me. I was very busy and hesitated to get on a call to talk about a deal that no longer existed. However, to keep the ball moving and get Harold and Lorna's house back on the market I took the call. The broker said that she imagined my clients were upset about the deal collapsing and was sorry, but that she would like to buy the house for her own family to live in.

"Are you kidding me?" I burst out, my surprise eclipsing my professionalism.

"No!" she said. "I am very serious." The new deal had the same terms and the same closing date. I could not get in touch with Harold and Lorna because they had already boarded the plane and were en route to New York. So I drew up a new set of contracts and faxed them to the broker, conditional on my clients' consent. When Lorna and Harold landed, I told them the good news. All Harold could say to his speechless wife was, "See, all that worry was for nothing. Nobody knows what the future will bring. It's all just one big Maybe!"

Getting Out of Bed in the Morning

> Everything that is done in the world is done by hope.
>
> —MARTIN LUTHER KING JR.

Some people believe that hoping for certain things to happen is an attachment that leads to suffering. They either seek to protect themselves by assuming the worst will come, or aim to cultivate neutrality toward the world, to protect themselves from the pain of disappointment.

I believe, though, that most of us would find it impossible to get out of bed in the morning without hope. Every business, every investment, every first date, and every other situation we embark on has hope packed into it. It is not hope that causes us emotional pain. Instead it is our inability to be flexible and fluid in the face of change and uncertainty. Maybe is the key to remaining free of our attachments that create suffering, while embracing hope for the future at the same time. Life may not go exactly as we planned, but there is always the hope that Maybe our path will still lead us to the life we desire.

Light a Candle and Send in the Clowns

> Don't curse the darkness—light a candle.
> —CHINESE PROVERB

What do Phineas Taylor Barnum, Henry John Heinz, Milton Snavely Hershey, Henry Ford, and Walt Disney all have in common? Believe it or not, each of these famous and successful entrepreneurs from history went bankrupt at least once while pursuing their dreams. Here are their stories.

The great American showman Phineas Taylor Barnum filed for bankruptcy due to losses he incurred in unwise business ventures. After bankruptcy and a bunch of learned lessons, he organized "The Greatest Show on Earth." In 1881, he merged his circus with that of his most successful competitor, James A. Bailey, under the name all of us know today: Barnum and Bailey Circus.

Henry John Heinz, condiment manufacturer, started his company in 1869 by selling horseradish, pickles, sauerkraut, and vinegar. In 1875, the company filed for bankruptcy due to an unforeseen bumper harvest that the company could not keep up with and thus could not meet its payroll obligations. Heinz immediately started a new company and introduced a new condiment, tomato ketchup, to the market. Everyone knows the name of his company, which was, and continues to be, very prosperous.

Born in 1857, Milton Snavely Hershey had only a fourth grade education, but he was certain he could make a good product that the public would want to purchase. He started several candy companies that failed, and filed for bankruptcy before launching what is now the Hershey Company. Clearly, his last attempt was a profitable venture.

We all know of automobile manufacturer Henry Ford. What not so many know is that Ford's first two automobile manufacturing companies failed. The first company filed for bankruptcy, and the second ended because of a disagreement with a business partner. In June 1903, at the age of forty, Ford created a third company, the Ford Motor Company, with a cash investment of approximately $30,000. By July of 1903, the company's bank balance had dwindled to $223.65, but then Ford sold its first car, and as they say, the rest is history.

Walt Disney, cartoon creator, filed for bankruptcy in the early 1920s after his company's main client went out of business. Disney said he could no longer pay his employees or the rent and had no choice but to file bankruptcy himself. Subsequently, he formed a new company with a loan from his parents and his brother. In 1928, he created Mickey Mouse, and the result was international success.

Just as a bankruptcy can be the darkest day for a business, there are times in our lives when we may feel that the darkness has taken hold. This is the moment when we can let Maybe help us search for the light. The light of Maybe has the power to guide us through the darkness to a place where we can once again find abundance, purpose, and joy in our lives.

TRY THIS
. . . . .

FEELING SAD,
BUT NOT FOREVER

Is it okay to feel sad, anxious, or disappointed? Yes. It is essential to living a full and authentic life that you allow yourself to feel your emotions . . . and allow them to shift. One of the best things about Maybe is that it does not demand you feel different about an experience or situation you are facing. Sometimes it is hard to see the positive side of life when you feel disappointed or when an unexpected event leaves you feeling alone and groundless. You want to feel optimistic, but you just don't see how life will change or what could possibly make things better. This is a perfect moment to let Maybe into your life. The idea of Maybe helps you accept where you stand in the moment, but also gives you an opening to recognize that things will always change.

So the next time you are feeling hopeless, miserable, or even just a little sad, try this. Simply notice and identify the feeling. Breathe. Say to yourself, "I am feeling miserable," or "sad," or however you would describe it. Breathe. Breathe some more. Now begin to notice when there is a shift in the feeling, however small. This is when you can allow the feeling, having been given its due, to pass away like a cloud breaking up in the sky. Now you can ask yourself, "What's left?" "What's next?"

Don't worry if it takes a while for the feeling to pass. Just be mindful that life is filled with possibility even if you can't feel it in the moment. In time, you understand that Maybe whatever situation is making you feel miserable or sad will turn out to be a good thing, Maybe things will get better, or Maybe the emotion will evolve into acceptance and feeling okay about how things turned out. Maybe allows you to have these feelings but will not let you get stuck in that place. It offers you an opening of hope that you can glide into naturally over time when you feel ready.

THREE

Maybe There Is Another Way

. . . . .

Linear Thinking

Perhaps you've already heard this story. It illustrates so well our tendency to get stuck thinking there's only one way out of a given situation that I think it bears repeating.

A flood came, and a man had to climb onto the roof of his house. As the waters rose, a neighbor in a rowboat appeared and told him to get in. "No," replied the man on the roof, "the Lord will save me." Then a firefighter appeared in a speedboat. "Climb in!" shouted the firefighter. "No," replied the man on the roof, "the Lord will save me." A helicopter appeared, and the pilot shouted that he would lower a rope to the man on the roof. "No," replied the man on the roof, "the Lord will save me." Eventually the man drowned and went to heaven, where he asked God why He hadn't helped him. God shrugged. "I sent a neighbor, a firefighter, and a helicopter. What more do you want?"

This story always reminds me of how we can get so stuck on the way we think a life experience should be that we can't see what is really in front of us. We surrender all other possibilities because we envision that our lives can unfold in just one way. I call this limited view on life "linear thinking."

Don't get me wrong. Linear thinking can be practical and beneficial when a situation has clear procedures that will help us achieve our goals. For instance, if we were to break a limb we would most likely go to a hospital and have a qualified doctor set it in an established procedure so it would heal properly. If we were constructing a building, we would follow established practices of material design so that the building does not collapse. However, unlike these examples, the path to achieving many of our goals can rarely be planned with an exact certainty. There are often many routes to success—some twisting, some circuitous, and some with hairpin turns that sneak up unexpectedly.

In the bigger picture, linear thinking tends to derail our goals. With our linear thoughts, we write stories in our minds about how our lives will unfold in the future or how our goals will be achieved. In order to alleviate our fears of uncertainty, we reinforce and cling to these stories, creating expectations that the events in our lives need to unfold exactly as we envision. These stories become so real in our minds that when our life experiences do not match them, we often become unhappy, devastated, and confused. But these stories we tell ourselves often have very little to do with our goals themselves. Instead they are fixed and finite thoughts about how our goals *should* come to fruition. These stories are mere illusions, and when they don't happen, our goals usually remain intact—simply waiting for us to achieve them in some other way.

Linear thinking leads us to believe that there is a right and a wrong way for our lives to unfold. How often, for instance, do we believe that we need to get a particular job or promotion in order to be going in the right direction? Or that a stock must go up for us to be financially secure. Or that we need to win a particular client to further our careers? How often have we yearned for a certain person to like us so that we can be happy? We tell ourselves story after story, believing we know how life should proceed for our well-being and success. But how can there be just one way for us to manifest our goals? Logically most of us would agree that there are many ways to achieve a particular goal, and yet emotionally we fail to live with this belief in our daily lives. When the emotional attachment to our stories defies logic, we fall into the linear thinking trap. And stay there, and stay there some more.

The philosophy of Maybe is a simple and effective way to let go of linear thinking. It frees us to pursue our goals with peace, joy, and vigor.

When we embrace the mind-set of Maybe, we are no longer hamstrung by these stories we've laboriously written for ourselves. As we realize that things may happen in many different ways, we begin to connect with all of the other possibilities that lie ahead of us. As we learn to sit with all these possibilities, our wisdom begins to guide us to the path of our greatest potential and fulfillment.

NYU or Bust!

Throughout college, I had my heart set on becoming an attorney. To satisfy my addiction to certainty, I convinced myself that attending New York University Law School was what I needed for my life to be fulfilling and complete. The thought of going to NYU Law School made me feel I had a plan that would guarantee me a great job and a successful career. In reality, I knew very little about the school and had never even visited it. So without any rational basis, this became my linear story: I would be going to law school at NYU.

I happened to be in New York City the day the response to my application to NYU was delivered to my family home on Long Island, New York. My father read me the letter over the telephone, and the outcome was that I had been wait-listed. A strangled "No" was all I could utter.

I ran crying through the streets of New York City that day as if my life was over. I had banked my whole future on this plan. When it didn't unfold that way, I felt like a caged animal with nowhere to go. In my mind the future was lost, and I felt that I was suddenly suffocating in my own skin; my future, my dreams, and everything I had wanted were now gone. Depleted and without hope, I walked over to NYU Law School. I sat on the curb in front of the main entrance and wept.

Once home, I did nothing for weeks and fell into great despair. So sure had I been that NYU was my only good option, I even let the acceptance dates lapse for the other law schools that had offered me admittance.

Then one day a friend asked me what I was doing when I graduated college, and I realized that I had absolutely no plans. I was set on the belief that if things did not go according to my plan, I would fade into oblivion. But here I was still breathing, eating, talking, and existing. I still existed, even without the linear story of how my life should take shape.

So how important, I began to wonder, was the story after all? Finally, it dawned on me that I still wanted to go to law school and become an attorney. It was just my own story of how it had to happen that was standing in my way. Within a few hours, I hopped on a train to Fordham Law School, one of the schools that had offered me admission. I walked into the admissions office and begged them to accept me after the deadline for my response had passed. Fortunately, they did. Fordham was not the school I had expected to attend, but it was a good, reputable school that served my real goal of becoming an attorney.

What's more, and what's so poignant and remarkable about this story for me is that, because I attended Fordham, the following events took place:

1. Through a friend at the school, I met and fell in love with the man who became my husband.
2. I met two of my closest friends there.
3. I got a job from a firm that employed many students from Fordham Law School, and—irony upon irony—they paid

for me to attend NYU Law School in the evenings to earn my Master of Law degree.

4. Several years later, I started my own law practice with the help of classmates from Fordham Law School.

So there I was. I had a law degree, my husband, friends, my own law practice, and an advanced law degree. Maybe it was a good thing I did not get into NYU in the first place!

Can you imagine all of the pain and suffering I could have avoided if I had seen my rejection from NYU not as a death knell, but as the beginning of something altogether new and positive in my life?

I would have bet anything on the day that I was wait-listed at NYU that my life was ruined. I had convinced myself that I needed to attend NYU to be successful because I wanted the validation and the certainty that my life was on the right track. I had been so busy pouting about how things had not gone well and using all of my energy telling my sad, linear story to everyone around me, that I almost missed the other opportunities available to me. My attachment almost cost me my true goal of becoming an attorney, not to mention all the other wonderful events that have happened to me as a result. I was very fortunate that I woke up before I missed such an amazing chance.

Step Away from the Door to See What's Possible

One day, I was watching the movie *Madagascar* with my children. There is a scene in the movie when a lion gets thrown out of the jungle and the other animals shut a door in his face. The lion starts to go crazy; all he wants to do is get back into the jungle, and he bangs and bangs on the door screaming, "Let me in! Let me in!" As my kids and I were watching the lion in total despair banging on the door, we started to laugh. Why? There was nothing on either side of the door. At any point in time, the lion could have moved to the left or the right or even on top of or below the door and entered the jungle, but he just kept banging. He could not see beyond the door right in front of his face. In his mind, straight ahead and through the door was the only way back into the jungle. Based on his past experience, he believed that because it was the portal through which he'd been thrown out of the jungle, it was the only way he could get back in.

After watching that scene, I understood why some of my clients, who loved the idea of Maybe in the abstract, had trouble moving past their linear thoughts. They were standing too close to the proverbial door of their businesses, their careers, or their lives. Sometimes the door was open and sometimes it was closed, but either way, they could not see beyond the door because they were standing right up against it. The door was blocking their view to any possible future other than that linear path to their desired outcome. Just like the lion from *Madagascar*, they failed to see that these doors had absolutely nothing around them but pure open space.

When I began to introduce the idea of the door to my clients, many started to visualize a place beyond it, and how simple it was to get there. When my clients were able to step back from the door, they realized that their path doesn't have to take them through the door—they can go around it and still get to their objective. Suddenly what seemed impossible was anything but, and a vast array of possibilities once again opened up.

Turn a Light On

It was September 2008 and the stock market was falling hundreds of points each day. People were losing their life savings. Retail sales were down considerably as people tried to survive the credit crisis. Around this time, my client John called me for a meeting. We had not spoken for a while, and he asked me to meet him at his elegant retail store in the heart of Manhattan. As I walked into the store, I marveled at the beautiful vintage furniture carefully placed along with artisan lamps that made the room glow. I saw John sitting in the back of the store, looking as though he had lost all the blood from his face. He told me that he had not paid the rent in three months, sales were down more than 80 percent, and he could not make payroll this week. On top of it all, he was being evicted from his apartment.

At first, I was taken aback. A store that had thrived for so long in Manhattan now barely had a pulse. John told me that he felt it was all over for him and that he would file for bankruptcy, pack up, and move back to his native country. I stopped him in the middle of his sentence and said, "John, let's just stop and breathe." In that breath, I realized that although things appeared grave at that moment, Maybe they were not as bad as they seemed. Maybe there was another way for him to do business and salvage everything he had worked so hard for over the years. John was standing in front of a very large closed door. He started his business with a retail store in Manhattan fifteen years earlier, and he could not imagine another path.

As John sat there breathing, I asked him to do the door exercise with me. He agreed.

John first placed his attention on the door that represented his retail store. He said standing in front of this door made him feel depressed and overwhelmed and that he had trouble catching his breath. I then asked him to focus on the door that represented going completely out of business and filing for bankruptcy. John felt no relief in front of this door either. He said the thought of bankruptcy made him feel lost. He felt a terrible longing for the business he worked so hard to grow and maintain. I then asked him to pull away from both doors and create an image of going beyond the doors into an open space called Maybe. I asked him during the visualization, "John, if you want to save this business, are you willing to believe that Maybe there is another way?" He said that he did not know but he would think about it. I asked John to do the visualization again in the evening.

John called me the next morning to say that he was ready to enter the field of Maybe because the way he was living and doing business was too painful and was, in his words, a closed door. He also did not want to file for bankruptcy. With courage amidst a swell of uncertainty, within three weeks John surrendered his space to the landlord and put all of his vintage furniture into storage. He moved his business to Brooklyn and decided to sell his artisan lamps on the Internet. He retained one salesperson and got more involved in the day-to-day business. There were a lot of tough decisions to be made, but he stayed within Maybe through it all. He began to believe that things could work out more than one way. He remained resilient and flexible.

One year later, with the practice of Maybe, John's business was again profitable and began to thrive. In fact, today John is happier than he has been in years. He does not feel stuck thinking that his life and business have to follow one certain path to be successful. He is now expanding the products he offers and working on creating his own furniture line.

Resistance Is Futile

> We must be willing to let go of the life we have
> planned, so as to accept the life that is waiting for us.
> —JOSEPH CAMPBELL

Deciding to stop banging on a closed door is not just about figuring out how to achieve your goals in another way; it is also about letting go of a great deal of emotional pain. There is a tremendous amount of pain involved in believing our lives can work out only if a door that is closed to us somehow opens. And arguing that things should be different than they actually are in any given moment is like banging your head against a closed door. As you read this, it may seem like common sense to not bang your head against a door. But how many times when an unexpected event that we don't like occurs in our lives do we say or think the following things:

"This should not be happening to me."
"Now that this happened, things can never work."
"That was my one chance, and now it is lost."
"If I could just go back in time and do it over again, my life would be right."

These familiar statements express the pain of a linear path gone wrong.

There are two reasons these types of thoughts create so much emotional pain. The first is that they are linear in nature and lead us to believe that our lives will be a success and that we will prosper in only one specific way. The second reason is that these thoughts make us believe that the experi-

It is so painful not to accept things as they are.

ence that we are having "should" not be happening. The latter creates a tremendous amount of resistance and can prevent us from seeing how our lives might grow and change as a result of an event we did not expect.

What if instead of resisting what we are experiencing, we embraced the idea of Maybe? What if we stopped arguing about why the situation is happening, why things are not working out as we planned, or why this person or that is doing something to us, and instead focus on what we can do about it? Maybe there is another way to resolve the situation, or Maybe there is another way to achieve the same goals, or Maybe it is time for our lives to take on a totally new direction.

It is *so* painful not to accept things as they are. As we embrace Maybe, the emotional pain we feel starts to dissipate because we are no longer arguing with the obstacle we face. I'm not saying that we have to like or prefer the experience that we are having, but accepting that it exists is the first step toward changing it. We have only so much energy and time to accomplish what we want in our lives. Arguing with what is can prevent us from finding another path to our success.

TRY THIS

· · · · ·

VISUALIZATION ON THE DOOR

Some of my clients enjoy doing visualizations. If you do too, I offer you the following techniques to embrace Maybe, which you can do either in your mind or, if you like a more concrete approach, with a pen and paper in hand, sketching out the images you see. These visualizations have proven very effective ways of training the mind to resolve problems, create new opportunities, and choose a different path.

To Resolve a Problem

To begin, close your eyes and see your particular problem as a door. Just sit for a minute or two and focus on the large door that lies in front of you. It may feel overwhelming or produce some anxiety, but try to stay still and breathe. The feeling you are having is an exaggerated feeling of the stress that has been going on in your mind and body as you have been dealing with this problem. Now imagine you are pulling away from the door. As you pull away, you will see how much smaller the door becomes, and you will realize that this door is standing alone, with nothing else around it. Start to take in the space around the door,

Don't resist what is, but and now focus your attention on

focus on what could be. that space. See the whole picture of

the white space around the door.

Keep moving around in the space. Feel the freedom of moving anywhere in the white space without being blocked. Now see the whole picture, including the door, and focus on the white bright space around it.

Name the white space Maybe, with all its possibilities.

Just stay there. Notice how small the door is compared to the space. Again, focus on the white space and the word "Maybe." Stay as long as you can or as long as you like.

This exercise will help you create alternatives beyond the door—new possibilities and new ideas to approach your problem in unexplored ways. If there is more than one problem in any given situation, then create more doors in the visualization. In the beginning of the visualization, spend some time with each door separately to gain a sense of how a particular problem is making you feel. After spending some time in front of each door, pull back and see them all within the vast open space of Maybe.

Start by doing this exercise for ten minutes in the morning

and ten minutes at night. Bring lightness into your life. Don't resist what is, but focus on what could be.

Creating New Opportunities

If you're seeking to create new opportunities and possibilities for yourself but are not sure what they might be, the following variation on the door visualization can be helpful. Close your eyes and think of all the things that you want for your life. Your thoughts might include topics such as love, friendship, a job, or money. Now, in your mind, create five doors for a single topic that you would like to focus on. Pick an emotion for each door that you would feel if you had exactly what you wanted in that area of your life. Don't worry if you have fewer than five emotions identified; you will still benefit from the visualization.

For instance, if you are thinking about finding a fulfilling new career but are not sure what it would be, imagine the emotions you would feel if you found it. These emotions could include joy, passion, fulfillment, security, or prosperity, but whatever they are they must come from within you. How would finding the right job actually make you feel? Now, after placing each emotion in front of a door, open each door within your mind and feel the white, infinite light of possibility flowing toward you. After focusing on each door, see them all together in a white space with white light pouring out of each door and merging with the open space that surrounds it. Stay in this open space for at least ten minutes. Feel the emotions that each door is pouring out to all of the possibilities in your life. Start by doing this exercise for ten minutes in the morning and ten minutes at night. You will start to connect to the space that allows you to open your life and leads to the fulfillment you want.

Choosing Which Path to Take

Sometimes we can't choose which path to take in our lives. The confusion prevents us from seeing all of the Maybes that lie within each decision. Again, the door visualization can be a powerful tool to help you find the way to the possibilities you seek. With your eyes closed, concentrate for one minute on your goal. Now, create a door for each choice that you are currently considering to achieve that goal. Visualize standing in front of each door for a few minutes. Note how each choice makes you feel. Try to connect to at least three to five emotions that come up for you in front of each door. Now open the door in question and see the wide-open white space within it. Feel the freedom inside the door and focus on the various emotions you are feeling.

Do this exercise for each choice before you. Now see all the doors in front of you and take in the open space all around them. Clear your mind and focus on your goal again. With that goal in mind, focus on the white, infinite space around each open door. Remain there as long as you comfortably can. Start by doing this exercise for ten minutes in the morning and ten minutes at night. As you continue to do this exercise, the choice that will connect you to your ultimate goal will become clear.

Keep going with these exercises and watch your life unfold with new choices and new possibilities.

FOUR

Let Go of the Past
(But Hold on to the Wisdom)

. . . . .

Two traveling monks reached a river where they encountered a young woman. Wary of the current, she asked if they could carry her across. One of the monks hesitated, but the other quickly picked her up onto his shoulders, transported her across the water, and put her down on the other bank. She thanked him and departed. As the monks continued on their way, the other one was brooding and preoccupied. Unable to hold his silence, he spoke out. "Brother, our spiritual training teaches us to avoid any contact with women, but you picked that one up on your shoulders and carried her!"

"Brother," the second monk replied, "I set her down on the other side, while you are still carrying her."

The Things We Carry

Linear thinking often dominates our thoughts when we are holding on to the past or old thought patterns. Our linear thoughts make us believe we know exactly how something will happen based on what happened yesterday, last week, or last year. This can be a helpful tool to guide us in our lives, but it can also be what keeps us experiencing the same painful and disappointing results.

Linear thinking is like a mathematical equation where we can keep adding up the sum of numbers, and no matter how many times we change the order of the numbers, we will always get the same sum over and over again. However, if we change just one number, even by a fraction, we will get a new result. Often, we imagine we are changing our lives by rearranging things differently, but as long as our actions are based on the same thoughts and patterns from our past, the results will most likely be the same.

So why do many of us choose the patterns of our pasts to dominate the decisions that we make in our lives? We rely on the past in an attempt to reduce the uncertainty in the present moment. We often choose the path of least resistance or one that is comfortable for us because of our fear of the unknown. However, this need for certainty results in a limited vision of possibilities that lie ahead in any given situation. The fear of uncertainty prevents us from seeing the freshness of the opportunities offered by each new moment because we are always looking at new occurrences in old ways in order to reproduce the safe and the known.

Once we embrace the philosophy of Maybe, our minds stop searching for a finite answer to each problem we are facing. Instead, we become curious and open to creating exciting new paths in our lives. We enter a new space filled with infinite opportunities and possibilities. By embracing Maybe, we can abandon thoughts and beliefs based on our past experiences and become change agents working toward new results. This is the true magic of "Maybe!"

Sitting on a Cold Stove

> We should be careful to get out of an experience
> only the wisdom that is in it, and stop there, lest we
> be like the cat that sits down on a hot stove lid. She
> will never sit down on a hot stove lid again, and

that is well; but also she will never sit down on a
cold one anymore.

—MARK TWAIN

When first introduced to the idea of Maybe, some of my clients worry that if they let go of their past experiences, they
will also be letting go of the wisdom they have gained along
the way.

However, exactly the opposite occurs when we embrace
Maybe—we connect with our true wisdom minus our fear.
The wisdom we've gained through our experiences is part of
the fiber of our being and cannot be lost. But fear of uncertainty clouds our wisdom by creating a distorted picture of
all we can truly learn from each experience. When we burden
our present and future with fears of uncertainty, we are no
different from Mark Twain's cat. We can become so focused
on avoiding what happened yesterday that we limit the possibilities in our lives. For most of us, our goal is not to re-create
or avoid our past experiences as much as it is to create the life
that we truly desire. We must trust our wisdom to help us
avoid the hot stove lids while we are exploring all the other
possibilities that exist for our lives.

Some simple examples of this could be our reaction to

getting bitten by a dog, falling off a ladder, or breaking our leg in a skiing accident. Should we, in the wake of such experiences, be afraid of animals, afraid of heights, afraid of sports, and avoid them at all costs? Or is the wisdom that we should know the dog before we pet it and still love animals, be more focused when we work on our roof and enjoy our love for working with our hands, and take a few skiing lessons to improve our skills and enjoy the adventures of nature?

Sometimes experiences in our lives are more complicated than these examples and it is difficult to pinpoint what happened in our past that is holding us back today from pursuing our goals. That is exactly why Maybe is so powerful. It doesn't ask you to figure out where the scar comes from; instead it allows you to open up and go forward regardless of what happened yesterday. Maybe acknowledges that uncertainty does not have to be a breeding ground for our fears, but instead can be fertile ground for our wisdom.

Brazilian Chicken

The way that past experiences can get in the way of a fresh opportunity reminds me of the story of my friend Keith. Keith lived in a large building in Manhattan. After living there for a few years, he began to run into a particular woman in the elevator. Finally, after a few months, Keith decided to ask her out. At the end of their lovely evening, he invited her back to his place. Keith really liked her and was excited that night about their blooming relationship. However, as soon as they got to his apartment, she explained to him that she was a Jehovah's Witness and tried to convert him. Keith was taken aback and ended the evening abruptly. Afterward, the woman continued to approach him in the hallway for a chance to convert him. After this experience, Keith decided that he would not talk to anyone in the hallways or elevators other than uttering a polite hello, if needed. He now believed it was a mistake to get involved with anyone on any level at the places where you live or work. Because of this one encounter, he became extremely uncomfortable living in the building and thought about moving.

About a year later, Keith started to frequent a Brazilian restaurant in the East Village once a week. He loved their food and especially a roasted chicken dish he ordered each time he was there. He also enjoyed speaking with a Brazilian waitress who worked there, a woman named Rosa.

He actually found himself thinking about her and the chicken before he arrived at the restaurant each Thursday night. He wanted to ask Rosa out but remembered how uncomfortable he felt living in his building after the incident with the other woman. Based on that experience, he felt that if he asked Rosa out, the date with her could end badly, and he would have to give up his visits to the restaurant and give up his delicious roasted Brazilian chicken. For this reason, Keith never asked Rosa for a date.

One day, Keith arrived at the restaurant and Rosa was gone with no forwarding information. His opportunity to date someone he liked had fled, traded for the certainty of a good meal. His lament for his lost opportunity lingered for months as he continued to go to the restaurant, still longing to see Rosa.

One evening, Rosa came by for a visit for the first time since leaving her job. Keith just happened to be in the restaurant that night, too. After not seeing Rosa for a few months, Keith's need for certainty felt a lot less important. He asked her out.

Today, they are married and enjoy a happy and loving relationship. One can argue that Keith and Rosa were "meant to be" or that Keith was just lucky that he saw Rosa again. Either way, it was Keith's past experience that at first prevented him from seeing the opportunity in front of him. The moment he decided not to ask Rosa for a date, he had chosen his need for certainty over the woman who ended up being the love of his life.

Many people might judge Keith's pattern as extreme or ridiculous, but I present his behavior as a simple example of how the past creates our patterns of thinking for the future. So many of the past experiences we have had in our lives have created these kinds of patterns or preconceived thoughts that stifle our judgment and make us overly cautious in the present. Most of us, at one time or another, have chosen the certainty of our own "Brazilian chicken" over an opportunity that could lead us on our path to great things.

Everyday Maybe

> We first make our habits, then our habits make us.
> —JOHN DRYDEN

Even when we understand the power of Maybe, we may very well continue to be unaware of the ways we repeat a habit of relying on the past for the sake of certainty. Often, because the experience we are having in the moment appears novel and new to us, we are totally unaware that we are responding to a situation based on something that happened to us yesterday or ten years ago. Yet the seeds of our past experiences lie dormant within us until an event evokes a memory or emotion from the past, eventually blooming into a familiar outcome. Some people spend years in psychotherapy searching for the origins of their suffering in order to create a new way of living. Others try alternative ways to nurture feelings and habits in order to diminish the old ones that have had such power over their daily lives. While both of these methods are valid choices, the philosophy of Maybe offers a simple way to achieve a new approach.

By saying Maybe to any given situation, we choose not to water the seed of an old habit, but instead open ourselves to all the possibilities that exist in each moment. The linear thought of how we "should" act or how an experience "should" be will not survive in the field of Maybe.

In Maybe, our minds settle into a place where we not only acknowledge that we do not know, we also feel good about not knowing. It is as if we are liberated from everything that has happened before in our lives, and we are brought to a new place where there is hope that our lives can be different. As Maybe becomes a daily practice, new seeds of hope, possibility, and creation flourish and the life you long for is born.

So how can we become aware of our habitual linear thinking when we are stuck in patterns from the past that limit our lives? How do we remember to say Maybe and look beyond things as we've always seen them? The easiest way to create the awareness or the new habit is to embrace Maybe as a daily practice.

It is amazing what creatures of habit most of us are. We eat the same foods, take the same route to work, and settle in to our daily routine with little variation or inspiration, day after day, month after month, and year after year. What if we regularly opened up to Maybe instead? Would we become more curious and try new things every day, like walking a different way to the train station, or eating something we've never tried before? And might those little breaks in our routine lead us to explore a new idea at work? Would we open up to a new opportunity in front of us, whether a new friend, a potential love interest, a promising job opening, or a fresh approach to communicating with friends and family? The more we embrace Maybe on a daily basis, the more our lives will reflect new possibilities. And the more Maybe becomes our daily practice, the more it will become a new habit. When we find ourselves stuck we will already be primed to utilize the tool of Maybe. In this way, we move forward in our lives with greater ease.

Practicing Maybe in the Elevator

The Maybe Mind is a daily exercise we can use to surrender how we think life *should* be and instead focus on all that it *can* be. Incorporating the Maybe Mind in our everyday routine is a great way to break the habit of our past patterns and linear thinking. The best way to engage the Maybe Mind on a daily basis is to make a plan every morning before getting out of bed or while getting ready to start the day. It is a commitment to say Maybe in response to certain situations that could arise throughout our daily interactions and experiences. You might be surprised how much more exciting and interesting a daily activity, work project, or communication with a friend can be when you stay curious and open to new paths and ideas.

Although I use Maybe all the time, I still enjoy doing the exercise of the Maybe Mind to discover areas of my life where I can be more open. This, in turn, helps me to continue to access more possibilities. Here is an example of an exercise I did a while back when I committed to the Maybe Mind.

I used to be extremely concerned with how others perceived me, and subsequently I found it hard to be at ease with people I didn't know well. A few days before Thanksgiving, I woke up in the morning and I decided that, instead of trying to control social situations as I'd done in the past, I would commit to use the Maybe Mind when I was in a situation with someone I did not know.

Later that afternoon, I was in the elevator with a woman from my building. She was in her late seventies, and I had seen her in the building before but we'd never spoken. I was carrying a cake for the Thanksgiving dinner I planned to host at my apartment. Breaking my habit of keeping to myself around new people, I said hello and asked how she was doing.

She responded, "I am good and old." She then remarked that I was holding a very big cake. I responded that it was for a Thanksgiving feast at my apartment in a few days. I had reached my floor and was holding the elevator door open with my foot. At that moment I again remembered my commitment to use the Maybe Mind when meeting someone new, so instead of interrupting our talk because I reached my floor I continued talking with her. I then asked her what she was doing for Thanksgiving.

"I have nowhere to go," she replied matter-of-factly.

Without hesitation, I asked if she would like to join us for dinner.

Her response was, "How can you invite me? I could be a thief!"

I looked at her cane and her sweet face and I laughed. "I think I'll take my chances," I said.

She accepted my invitation. Sure enough, the woman from the elevator, whose name is Jenny, came to Thanksgiving dinner with my family. She was a delight. I truly enjoyed her keen sense of humor and having her at my home. Since then we have spoken several times, and she has invited me to a few events honoring her late husband. She will be coming over for an upcoming holiday.

Thanks to Maybe, Jenny found joy in celebrating the holidays once again, and I embraced a chance to make a new friend.

The Maybe Mind at Work and Play

When we use the Maybe Mind at work, our openness to other people's thoughts and opinions leads us to a deeper understanding of where they are coming from and allows us to enter a more creative state to accomplish mutual goals. Instead of sticking to the way things have always been done, try to notice the opportunities, even small ones, for trying a new approach. Maybe a monthly meeting could be held in a more informal space. Maybe opening the floor to questions would yield some new ideas. Maybe a longtime office rival could be included in a new project rather than elbowed out— what would happen then?

Committing to engage Maybe when we are with our children, too, can be a lifesaver. Kids' behavior is unpredictable, and when we engage in Maybe we let go of how we think an experience should be or how our children should be acting. We can remain focused on what the children need to accomplish or where the family needs to go, but realize that there are many different ways to get there.

For example, every morning when I wake up, I commit to Maybe when I deal with my family. One of the most common challenges in my house is trying to get everyone up and out in order to be at school and work on time. Recently, my husband came back from the gym with ten minutes left on the clock before we had to leave for a concert. My older daughter was upset that she could not find her pants, and my younger daughter had decided to take photographs of her stuffed animals instead of brushing her teeth. I knew from experience that if I started to argue with anything that was happening in that moment, I would lose my way, become upset and worried, and end up leaving even later. Instead, I took a deep breath and remembered my commitment to Maybe. I thought to myself: Maybe we will get it together and leave on time, Maybe we can take a cab instead of walking, Maybe the event will start late, or Maybe being a few minutes late is not so bad.

I stayed calm in Maybe with all its possibilities. I directed my husband into the shower and reiterated the time that we needed to leave. I helped my older daughter find her pants with grace and ease and nudged my younger one to the bathroom to brush her teeth. We left the apartment ten minutes after I'd wanted to, but there was no worry, stress, or fighting. Walking out the door, we were all smiling. When we got to the concert, it turned out the start of the performance was delayed by ten minutes. We ended up being five minutes early!

The Maybe Mind can also help us stay present in our relationships with our spouses or good friends because it allows us to give up how we thought things "should" be and find a new place to be together. Instead of "That's not what I had in mind" or "That doesn't work for me," we find ourselves saying, "Maybe we can find a place that we both like to go,"

"Maybe we had a misunderstanding and we can try to meet and work it out," or "Well, I never thought of going there before, but Maybe it will be fun."

Our relationships become more open and flowing because we let go of our set ways and are more agreeable to the mishaps and mistakes we all make, as well as the new experiences our openness leads us to.

It's also worthwhile to commit to the Maybe Mind in everyday situations, like when we are food shopping, at a restaurant, at the gym, or waiting for the cable guy to show up. You'll spare yourself and others a lot of stress, and you'll expand your life in ways you never dreamed possible.

TRY THIS
. . . . .

ENGAGING IN THE MAYBE MIND

Before you go to sleep at night or early in the morning, make a commitment to engage in the Maybe Mind at some time during the day. You can start by picking an activity, work project, or interaction with your children, spouse, or friend. Now commit to saying Maybe in these situations or interactions when you feel yourself shutting down or not being adventurous or available to something new. It can be as simple as ordering something new for lunch, trying a new activity with your child after school, or keeping an open mind toward a coworker.

Track the results, and your feelings about these interactions or activities, in a journal, or just review them for yourself at the end of each day. Were you more lighthearted during the experience? Did you learn something new about the situation or about yourself? How did the situation work itself out? Do you think it would have been different had you not used the Maybe Mind?

Over time, you might just find that life with Maybe is more open, interesting, and rewarding as you continue to reach out to new opportunities each and every day.

FIVE

The Present Is the True Gift

. . . . .

There is a Swedish proverb that says, "Worry often gives small things a large shadow." Many of us are conditioned to plan for a negative outcome, and if a positive outcome occurs, then we tend to believe it was "worth" the worry. However, living in a constant state of expecting bad things to occur in the future or assuming things will not go our way results in anxiety and stress and can ultimately make us sick.

I call this state of mind the *Negative Twist*. The Negative Twist is another form of linear thinking. It is a place in our minds where every bad thing that can happen actually does. We live out each miserable scenario in our minds, and become prisoners of our thoughts. Just like other forms of linear thinking, the Negative Twist limits our ability to create new possibilities for the future. What's more, the Negative Twist takes us out of the present moment. We get so consumed by this mind-set that we become oblivious to the actual world that is present around us. We rob ourselves of the true enjoyment of life as we are living it.

A Pathway Back to the Present

Maybe is an incredibly powerful tool to combat the Negative Twists we create in our minds. Almost instantly, Maybe can provide us with an easy pathway back to the present. As soon as we enter into the place of Maybe, the burden of stress and worry is lifted, and we can enjoy our lives in the moment. Maybe gives us the opportunity to truly be with our families and friends because we are not wasting time surmising what will happen tomorrow.

The idea of Maybe can bring our minds into "no thought." This state of "no thought" happens because, as we embrace Maybe, our thoughts dissipate and our negative stories about the future dissolve into the present. We can sit comfortably in the moment knowing that the future can unfold in many ways and Maybe not turn out as bad as we imagined.

For a spiritual seeker, "no thought" is aligned with the idea of inner peace. It is a state of being where we can truly experience what is before us in life with acceptance and tranquility. For many of my business clients, this idea of "no thought" means not worrying about their business and the future. For someone with personal issues, "no thought" can be not worrying about their kids or financial problems. Whatever the interpretation of "no thought" is, Maybe can bring us there. When Maybe frees us of all of our Negative Twists, there is truly nothing else to think about. The mind empties into the present with nothing to do and nowhere to go. In this way, we experience the present moment more fully.

Missing All the Birthday Parties

Years ago, my father told me a story about his friend Jack. Jack was unable to enjoy the fruits of his endeavors throughout his life because he was so focused on worrying about the future. One Friday afternoon when he wasn't in his office, Jack got a call from a client. Jack was in the steel construction business, and the caller was the owner of a building Jack's company was working on. The owner said that it was imperative that Jack get back to him as soon as possible. This was before cell phones, and when Jack called his client back, there was just an answering service to take his call. Unable to speak with his client, Jack concocted a story in his mind that, in order for a client to call and say it was imperative, something horrendous must have happened on the job site. It had rained and was windy on that Friday, and Jack decided in his mind that a steel beam had fallen and caused irrevocable damage, maybe even killing someone. Jack's steel crew had not worked that day because of rain, so they had no information to give him. Since his client had an unlisted number at his home residence, Jack did not have anyone to call to verify the catastrophe.

Jack didn't sleep most of that night. Every Negative Twist consumed his being. The next morning, Jack drove over two hours to get to the job site. When he arrived, there was nothing wrong. The steel structure was in place, and he drove two hours back to his home. As a result, Jack missed his son's birthday party. Still uncertain as to why his client had called, Jack conceived other Negative Twists in his head. He convinced himself he would be penalized by the owner for other subcontractors' mistakes or that the owner of the building was going bust and could not pay him. Finally, after a week-end of little sleep and terrorizing himself with these Negative Twists, Jack was finally able to contact his client on Monday morning. Jack braced himself for the worst. However, all he heard was that his client wanted to meet him that afternoon in order to give him an additional job and expedite the process of getting another building under construction as soon as possible.

This is how Jack lived most of his life. He had missed so much because he was not present enough in the moment to experience it. What Jack needed was the simple expression of Maybe to curtail the Negative Twists stemming from that telephone call from his client. But he never allowed himself to think that Maybe something good would happen. And yet no matter how much he worried about tomorrow, there was never anything conclusive in the moment to warrant his negativity. All Jack would have had to do was stay in that open place of Maybe until the veil of the unknown lifted and he could move forward. While he was waiting, he could have enjoyed those birthday parties, his wife, his kids, and all the other blessings in his life.

**Finding the Sweetness in Life
Even When Times Are Tough**

Don't get me wrong. I understand that the present is not always easy. Just because we are present doesn't automatically mean that we'll be happy. But it does allow for that possibility!

A man walking across a field encountered a tiger. He fled, and the tiger chased after him. Coming to a cliff, he caught hold of a wild vine hanging from a tree and swung himself over the edge. The tiger sniffed at him from the edge of the cliff. Terrified, dangling, the man looked down. Far below, another tiger had come and was waiting to eat him. Meanwhile, from the tree branch above him, two mice, one white and one black, little by little began to gnaw away at the vine. Suddenly, amidst all of this, the man noticed a luscious strawberry growing out of the edge of the chasm. Grasping the vine in one hand, he reached out and plucked the strawberry with the other and ate it. How sweet it tasted!

I remember hearing this story when I was young but I never really understood it. I never understood why anyone would eat a strawberry when he or she should be trying to escape the tigers! It wasn't until years later that I finally got it.

I had just found out my mother had breast cancer, and I was walking to meet her for dinner. My mind was seized by the most frightening thoughts of losing my mother and what this illness would mean. Panic overcame me. All of a sudden, a beautiful breeze hit my face and an enveloping peace and joy ran through me. Was it okay for me to feel this joy when danger was looming over my family? And then I realized, aha! This is the strawberry. I got to dinner, and the peace and joy stayed with me. My mother and I held hands and we laughed and cried a bit. And throughout that evening the depth of my joy was profound. I was acutely aware that in that moment there was nothing else to do but be present with each other. Sure, there would be a time to act on her illness and decisions to be made, but at that moment it was time to eat the strawberry. How sweet it tasted!

I am sure you realize that the story stops after the man eats the strawberry because the message of this story is to be in the moment. But my Maybe Mind says, "Hey, we have no idea what happens to the man. He could fall to his death after he enjoys the strawberry, but Maybe he is saved by a friend, or Maybe the tiger leaves for other prey or the man

Staying in the present is like opening the window to life.

figures out another way out of the situation." Adding hope and possibility to the story makes it easier to enjoy the strawberry and at the same time be aware that new possibilities can arise. This is when we realize that the unexpected can be our friend. It always brings change and change offers us not just obstacles but also new ways to move forward.

So whatever you are facing today, whether it is financial troubles, illness, or another crisis, be sure to find the strawberries when you can. This is the true essence of being alive, no matter what the future brings. Staying in the present is like opening the window to life. Maybe when you are not even looking the winds will change, offering you a way out of whatever you are experiencing.

The Essence of Maybe

One today is worth two tomorrows.
—BENJAMIN FRANKLIN

For me, the most profound aspect of Maybe is the sense of *presence* that it adds to our lives. The presence that Maybe brings alleviates so much emotional pain and allows us to feel the true essence of life as it is happening. Maybe enables us to do less worrying and more living. When our minds are empty of all the clutter, confusion, and thoughts of our daily lives, we start to notice things differently. We notice nature, our food, and our conversations with other people all with a new sense of discovery and understanding. It is as if we are coming out of a tunnel and we see the vivid colors of our lives for the first time. This new presence allows us to become more creative and innovative in response to the same ideas or problems that we have been dealing with for a long time. As we empty our minds there is more room for new ideas and concepts to come and go. We are on a new playing field where there is a peace and tranquility in the moment with all things that have been, that are, and that will be.

TRY THIS

· · · · ·

THE GIFT OF THE PRESENT

Each day we experience a wide range of emotions. Some are pleasant, and others make us miserable and stressed. It's often a Negative Twist that brings about these unpleasant emotions.

This exercise can be used on a daily basis to alleviate the Negative Twists your mind engages in and bring yourself back into the present, where you will be able to enjoy your work, your conversations, your lunch, your family, your friends, and everything else you experience in each moment. The future may be uncertain, but remember—Maybe it will be good. So enjoy the present. It is the true gift of life!

1. When you become aware that your emotions are negative during the day, whether you feel anxiety, stress, anger, or sadness, ask yourself what this particular Negative Twist is really about. Is it related to something that happened at work, or a fight with a loved one? Is someone you love ill? Try to find the source of the emotions that you are experiencing.

2. Now ask yourself the following. Are your emotions negative in the moment because you fear that what you are experiencing will never change or get better? Are your emotions negative because you are afraid that what is happening today will lead to an unhappy or unwanted result in the future?

3. As you did in the exercise in Chapter 1, ask yourself: Is it at all possible that Maybe things can work out differently

than you are projecting? Whether you think in this moment the answer is yes or no, close your eyes, breathe in deeply, and think to yourself, "Maybe there are possibilities out there that will help me change these circumstances." Now, breathe out and think to yourself, "Maybe things will change, and Maybe they will get better." Continue with this for a few minutes. Try to keep your eyes closed as you breathe slowly and feel the possibilities of Maybe in your entire body. If you need to stay with the breathing longer to calm your mind further, feel free to do so.

4. When you are done with the breathing exercise, open your eyes, and you will find your mind is clear and calmer. Now try to focus on your surroundings. What is happening right now in your life? Is the sun shining? Are you with people whose company you enjoy? Are you walking? Are you about to eat something? Are you grateful for what is currently going on? Feel the peace of not being as worried. Focus on life as it is happening.

The Reverse Maybe

> A person is not old until their regrets take the place of their dreams.
>
> **—PROVERB**

We are taken out of the present not only when we worry about the future, but also when we worry about the past—fretting over choices that we now regret. People who come to see me often share the belief that if they had made different choices in the past, things would be better today. They tell me about the missed business opportunity or the potential spouse that got away, or the job offer they wish they had taken. Could different choices have been wonderful and filled my clients' lives with joy? Yes. But it is also possible that the opportunity would have created other issues in their lives—the woman or man who got away would have meant a rocky and unpleasant relationship, and the job may have ended after the first week. All these stories actually do is keep us living in the past and out of the present.

Regret is a Reverse Maybe. It is a mind trap that keeps us reliving a pain we can never soothe. There is no external remedy for regret because it is merely a linear story that exists solely within us. Regret is a story we make up about how our lives could have been better if we had made another choice—but in reality, we don't really know what life would have looked like if we had made that choice, and we never will. The twists and turns of life might have taken us to other unexpected places, and Maybe not at all for the better.

Once we are able to realize that regret is just a fictitious story of what could have been, we can start to view our lives differently. Without the story of regret filling our minds with chatter, we can allow ourselves to be softer toward our past and more engaged in the now. Dropping regret gives us permission to rejoice and appreciate what we have accomplished in our lives and the love that we have shared with others. Without regret, we can look firmly at our lives today and discover all that is possible going forward. And even if we need to change direction, we can enter a new dialogue of "How do I really want to live?" without the anchor of yesterday holding us back and making us feel that we "missed our chance."

All we can know for sure is that everything that has happened before in our lives has brought us to *this* moment. Within this moment there is no regret. There is only the hope that Maybe we can create the lives that we want from this point forward.

Freedom from the Past

Recently, my client Cliff told me his business was really picking up and he had some ideas for new products. We had a great discussion about his ideas, and he will be pursuing a few of them in the near future. Then the conversation took an interesting turn. He told me that he had so much regret in his heart that it was eating him alive. His mother had passed away more than a year ago, and he had been struggling financially when she was alive. He regretted not having found his business success earlier so he would have had more money to take care of her and she could have shared in the joy of his success. I immediately understood and identified with the feeling of wanting to make our parents proud and see them happy. However, there was a huge piece of the picture getting blocked by all of Cliff's regret.

About ten years earlier, Cliff had moved back in with his mother after struggling financially for a long time. At that time, Cliff's mother became ill. Cliff took good care of her, taking her to doctor appointments, cooking for her, managing her medications and anything else that she needed. At one point she had pneumonia and might not have recovered if Cliff had not been there for her.

After sitting for a while with him, I said, "Cliff, you are stuck in a Reverse Maybe." He looked at me, puzzled. I went on, "You are rewriting a story about what might have been if you had a more successful business at that time. But, you have no idea what your life and your mother's life would have looked like if that had been the case. You might have been so busy with all of your work and success that you might not have had the time to take such good care of her; she might never have recovered from that bout of pneumonia so many years ago. You might have been so busy that you would have missed out on all of your time together. Yes, she might have had a few more fancy handbags, but that could never have taken the place of the quality time you spent together. Maybe you were exactly where you needed to be then and you are exactly where you need to be now. So, enjoy your current success and know that your mother was blessed to have a loving, devoted son like you."

Cliff looked at me with tears in his eyes. He recognized in that moment that he had no idea what his life would have been if his business had become more successful years ago. But he knew that he had taken very good care of his mother. This change in thinking won't change how much he misses his mother, but it allowed Cliff to move forward without looking back and constantly questioning what might have been.

GET OUT OF REVERSE

Identify a few experiences from the past that still make you feel regretful, unhappy, or hopeless. Ask yourself the following questions: "Am I absolutely certain that things would be better today if I had made a different decision during that experience?" "How do I know that it wouldn't have caused me other problems or an outcome I do not want?" Try to acknowledge that Maybe the decision you regret would *not* have turned out better had you taken a different course, may not have been better for reasons that you can't even imagine today.

In this moment, call to mind the things and people in your life that you most enjoy and cherish. Have you accomplished things in your life that you are proud of? Do you have relationships that are meaningful to you? Would they all be in your life today had you made another decision besides the one you are regretting? Maybe the things you cherish most in your life are with you in the present because of the decisions that you have made.

Repeat the following to yourself: "All I know is that everything that has happened in my life has brought me to this moment. Within this moment I let go of my regret and embrace the hope that Maybe I can create the life I want from this point forward."

SIX

Maybe Is Always at Play

. . . . .

Many years ago when I was practicing law, I used to wonder why some of my clients who suffered severe setbacks, such as having to sell their business or file bankruptcy, were able to recreate themselves and become successful again while others were not. One could argue that the difference between these clients was just the luck of the draw, a random stroke of good fortune, or being in the right place at the right time. Eventually, through watching enough people face difficulties both personally and in business over the years, I realized that those who sustain an ability to grow year after year or to rebound from a huge financial setback hold one common belief. They are people who believe that the field of possibilities is always infinite—*under all circumstances at all times.*

Sometimes a client will comment to me that the economy has changed or the way that he or she does business has changed and therefore there are no new possibilities to explore. In some sense, these clients are correct in their assessment, because when they see their businesses in a linear way their possibilities are limited. Their views may be chained to the past based on how they did business yesterday, a month ago, or a year ago. However, even though events in our lives are always changing, our awareness of the infinite possibilities of Maybe is a constant to help us deal with the ever-changing canvas of our lives. Within Maybe, the possibilities may change, but there are always plenty of options to choose from if we are willing to let go of what we have come to think we know. It is not about letting go of our wisdom; it is about letting go of our past, our fears, and our belief that life has only one lane. When my clients shift their belief systems and embrace the mind-set of Maybe, they find many avenues with new possibilities for success.

Other clients have challenged me on the validity of Maybe by protesting their dislike for any new possibilities. "I loved my business or my life the way it was before," a client would say. "Now it is gone, and the only possibility that can ever make me happy again is gone with it." Unable to see the forest for the

Maybe works anytime, anywhere, and under all circumstances if you give it a try.

trees, these clients could not get past the fear that they might never get their old life back. But, once a door closes, the only passageway to regain what we had or to start something wonderful is to embrace the uncertainty before us. Maybe is a lifeboat we can travel in as we search out new ideas and concepts. Even if an opportunity in front of us may not seem as good as the one that was before us last week or last month, it does not mean that it won't lead us to something new and amazing.

Maybe doesn't ask us to compare the past to the future, but instead helps us see where we are in life and supports us to explore what is possible. If we have the courage, we can continuously travel into uncharted territory without trepidation about the unknown.

The big message here is that Maybe works anytime, anywhere, and under all circumstances if you give it a try.

The Art of Maybe

I will never forget a party I attended a few years back. To my surprise, a friend of mine, Alan, showed up. I was surprised because I knew he had been depressed for more than a year and was generally out of the social loop. I had tried to approach him several times, but he clearly did not want to speak or have any contact. I surmised at the party that Alan had resigned himself to some sort of social communications, and this event gave us the chance to speak. With some reservation, he said to me, "You know that I've been depressed since the economy went into recession. My business has significantly declined. I no longer have any way of conducting business because the economy has changed so much." He paused for a moment, and then went on a rambling account of his demise as he saw it, based on Maslow's hierarchy of needs, the idea that unless our most basic needs are met we cannot attend to higher needs such as happiness and self-actualization.

Before the economic decline, Alan was an extremely successful art collector and ran a hedge fund buying and selling art. For me, the most amazing thing about Alan had not been his success in the art world but his positive attitude. He used to tell me that he was born under a lucky star. He used to say that there were always opportunities for him, and he would always find his way through any of life's obstacle courses. Then, when the financial crisis struck in September 2008 and the art world, just like many other asset-based businesses, went into a tailspin, so did Alan. With the world he knew gone, he could not see how he could fit his business into the new economy. He had come to believe all his possibilities were limited.

As he tried to convince me his failure was based on Maslow's theory of hierarchy of needs and it was beyond his control, I interrupted and, unable to contain myself in the face of my friend's despair, asked him, "Alan, what makes you think the field of possibilities is limited? Is the outside world dictating how you see your life? Did you ever consider that the field is unlimited but the possibilities in the field have changed? Did you ever consider that there's an entire world out there for you that you haven't even given a chance? Did you ever consider the fact that your whole entire life has been built on this theory and the only difference between you now and last year is that you stopped believing in the unlimited field?"

Alan paused and looked at me as we stood in silence.

I caught my breath, worrying I had not been gentle enough with him. Finally, Alan spoke.

"Allison, you know, you're right! I don't believe that all things are possible anymore. I created the hedge fund and just because it doesn't really work anymore, I've been putting everything on hold. All that happened is that my possibilities changed. That doesn't mean the playing field is limited."

In that moment, I could see a glimmer of the old Alan. He continued, "I once thought about becoming an art adviser and helping people buy and sell art. Maybe that can work or Maybe something else will. I think Maybe I need to go back to what I know, and feel all the possibilities that exist for me." We hugged and parted ways.

About two weeks later I was walking down the street when Alan came running up to me, screaming, "Allison, you saved me!"

I laughed, and had an inkling he'd found a way to get back on his feet. "No way! Whatever happened, you saved yourself. I just told you what you had forgotten."

It turns out that Alan woke up the next day after the party and started to believe again in the unlimited field of Maybe. It was so comfortable for him, like putting on a favorite pair of shoes. A few days later he ran into a woman who was an interior designer, someone with whom he had been trying to make a business connection for a long time. Alan said to her, "We should do business together. There are an infinite amount of opportunities for us to share."

Her response was that she had a client that might need an art adviser, and by the end of that week, he landed a major client with a twenty-five-thousand-square-foot home and empty walls, a person who yearned for his art advice. He also started calling outside the art world to people who owned commercial buildings to ask if they needed an adviser. He got some great responses that landed him more big clients. Now, he is busy every day, not as a hedge fund guy, but as an art adviser lending his expertise to the acquisition of artwork for corporations and private collectors. He is still not making as much money as he did at the height of the market, but he is making a good living, and he sees this as just the beginning of endless possibilities.

Where We Stand

On occasion, a client who is having difficulty embracing the concept of new possibilities will challenge the validity of Maybe by arguing that bad things happen in life. He or she will enter my office listing off the worst tragedies they can possibly think of from history, or a horrible event from the news, or a story that they heard from a friend. "What's the silver lining of Maybe in any of these situations?" I'm invariably asked.

I respond by saying that Maybe does not minimize hardships, nor does it ask us to pretend that life does not have its challenges. Instead, Maybe is a life philosophy that asks us to embrace all that is possible from where we currently stand. It offers us hope that, whatever we are facing in life, there may be a path for us to move forward and find another way to create new opportunities, live with less emotional pain, and find peace in the moment. After an event occurs, the field of Maybe exists for us to engage in thinking about what's possible. Yes, life will keep shifting, but that does not mean we are limited and cannot keep up with the changing tides. If we continuously stay in the open space of Maybe, our lives will evolve because we will be availing ourselves of all possibilities. Our focus becomes less about what is *not* happening and more about what can happen. If there is breath in us, then there is hope that whatever we are experiencing we will keep growing, and Maybe we'll find our way back to the joy of living.

Watering the Flowers

Cheryl is a landscaper in Manhattan who was recommended to me for some work on my terrace. The first few times I met Cheryl, she was very focused on her work and seemed preoccupied with other thoughts, so we didn't speak much. On her third visit to my apartment, I found Cheryl crying into the flowers she was planting for me. I asked her what was wrong, and she apologized profusely for her emotional state, finished planting, and abruptly left.

The next time I knew Cheryl was coming, I prepared some tea before she arrived and asked her to join me before she began her work. As Cheryl and I began to speak, she told me that her business partner, who was also her boyfriend of seventeen years, had left her a few months ago. She was devastated both emotionally and professionally. She was not only alone in her personal life, but she also had to deal with working without the man that she had loved for so long. She admitted that their relationship had been difficult and rocky at times, but it was what she knew and relied on. She said, "Look at me. I am now in my late forties. Who is going to love me at my age? Who is going to want to work with me? No one. I lost the love of my life, and now I have to go the rest alone."

There was a long pause in our conversation. I knew I had to challenge Cheryl's linear story on love, but I didn't want to disregard her feelings of loss, which I deeply respected. So I approached Maybe from a business perspective at first, hoping Cheryl would see that the uncertainty of her current situation could offer her many possibilities. She was telling a story of doom and gloom because she never expected to be left alone to run the business herself. However, as we discussed the unlimited possibilities of Maybe, she saw that she was no longer restricted by her partner's perspective and could branch out into other types of landscaping. She might be able to take on a new partner and have a more stable business. Or maybe something else would happen that neither of us could even imagine at that moment. Cheryl's adventurous spirit and passion for her work enabled her to embrace the idea of Maybe. She said, "I'll try it. I have nothing to lose." After she finished her work and was leaving, I said, "Cheryl, you might want to try the idea of Maybe with love as well." She looked at me and laughed as she walked out the door.

I saw Cheryl about three months later. She entered my apartment with a big smile. She told me that she had been using Maybe constantly since the last time that we had spoken. "I feel like a fifty pound weight has been lifted off me," she said.

Her stress about work had decreased, and she'd landed a few new clients. Also, after about seven weeks of living in Maybe, she was working at the National Arts Club near Gramercy Park planting flowers when she saw the back of a man carving flowers into the cement of the building. She thought how much she loved his work and thought Maybe she should tell him. Without even seeing his face, Cheryl yelled out, "Hey, I love your work." The man turned around and smiled, and she was surprised by how cute he was. They spoke for about an hour, and he asked for her number.

Normally, she would have said no, but she thought about Maybe and gave her number to the flower carver, whose name was Steve. She said the best part about meeting Steve that day was that she felt something speaking with him that she had not felt since her boyfriend left her—the chance of something wonderful. She was glowing the rest of the day. The next day she was standing on a tall ladder taking down Christmas lights from some trees about five miles away in upper Manhattan when she heard someone calling her name. It was Steve, the guy she met the day before. He was working on a job right next to her. She thought, what are the chances of running into the same person two days in a row in a city of eight million people? She smiled because she knew that such a possibility existed in the now familiar field of Maybe.

At the time of this writing, Cheryl and Steve have been together almost a year and she is extremely happy. In fact, her relationship with Steve is calm and pleasant instead of rocky and chaotic. He also helps her out on some of her busy days planting in the city. Cheryl says she now looks forward to maybe retiring with Steve down south in a few years, maybe living on a farm growing flowers and vegetables all year round, and watering them with love instead of tears.

The Moonless Night

> Once there was a Zen student who was with his master for many years. When the master felt he was going to die, he wanted to make even his death a lesson. One moonless night, the master took a torch, and with his student, set off through the forest. Soon they reached the middle of the woods where the master extinguished the torch without explanation. "What's the matter?" asked the student. "This torch has gone out," the master replied and walked on. "But," shouted the student, his

voice filled with fear, "will you leave me here in the dark?" "No! I will not leave you in the dark," returned the master's voice from the surrounding blackness. "I will leave you searching for the light."

—ADAPTED FROM *JACOB THE BAKER*
BY NOAH BENSHEA

If we have trouble finding Maybe the minute something unexpected happens in our lives, we should not worry. As long as we are aware that Maybe there's another way besides the one we fear, we will keep searching in the open space for other possibilities and will eventually find our way. As long as there is Maybe in our lives we will feel comfort that there is possibility and hope.

Everyone has moonless nights. I have developed a very intimate relationship with Maybe, and there are still times when something unexpected happens and I get anxious and need some time to reconnect to Maybe. I do some of the exercises or meditations in this book and check in to see if I am grasping at certainty. Time and again, when I fully embrace Maybe, I am able to deal with the twists and turns of life with peace of mind and find opportunities I never knew were possible. I have learned through my experiences that Maybe never leaves us, although we sometimes choose to leave it! Maybe is always there to guide us back and show us the way to new possibilities in our lives.

Giving It Up for Maybe

If you are still having a hard time finding Maybe after doing some of the exercises I've provided, you might have better luck if you try giving Maybe to someone else. The gift of Maybe provides so many people with a tremendous amount of hope. Keep in mind, too, that one of the biggest features of Maybe is that we never know exactly what it's going to look like or how it's going to come to fruition.

Let me share an example. About four years ago, I decided I was going to coach Robert, a homeless man who spent part of his days begging on a corner in downtown Manhattan. I had already established a routine with Robert over the span of about a year. I would give him some money when I passed him in my car, and when I was on foot, I would stop to chat with him to get to know him a little. Without ever calling it that, I began to offer him some coaching advice. In my first real conversation with Robert, I asked what he did for a living and offered my help. He indicated that he was an artist, and he was on the street because he had trouble selling his art. So

I told him to bring me some of his art and I would buy it. Robert responded that I might not like his work, and I told him not to worry and looked forward to seeing it. We agreed to meet on a Monday at 2 p.m. the following week. Surprisingly, Robert remembered our meeting, but when I showed up, he did not have any of his art with him. He said that the police had seized his paintbrushes, but he would be sure to bring his art to me the next week. Robert and I repeated this episode for about two months. His excuses ran the gamut from the rain having ruined his canvases to someone having stolen his art and so on. After a while, I realized that Robert might not have any art to bring.

I asked Robert about his occupation before he became homeless. He said he was an office manager in the construction business. He had been laid off years ago and had trouble finding new work. I suggested that maybe we could work to help him get a job in construction so he could get off the streets. To my surprise, Robert said that he had a résumé and would bring it the following Monday at 2 p.m. So, once again, we met. This time, he came without his résumé. Monday after Monday, Robert did not bring the résumé. Some days, his excuse was that he'd forgotten the résumé, and other days, that the rain ruined the résumé. These stories continued for a while, and I realized his résumé would never materialize.

My next step was to contact a friend who was a homeless advocate to gather some information regarding temporary and permanent housing programs in the city. Robert's response to every suggestion I made was either that he had already tried that route or that his girlfriend could not stay with him in any apartment and so he did not want to move off the street. In the face of each excuse, I checked with my friend the advocate and learned that none of Robert's responses about the limitations of a given program were accurate.

At this point, I finally knew it was time to stop. I was trying to push myself on Robert and, clearly, not really helping him. A few days later, after I had my realization, I was driving my car and saw Robert walking down the street away from his usual corner. He was not begging. He was just walking. I stopped my car, opened the window, and gave Robert one dollar. Robert replied, "Thanks! I was walking to get a cup of coffee and was hoping Maybe somebody would give me a dollar for it."

I laughed to myself. All this time I had been trying to create a "Maybe" for someone else. But the only Maybe Robert had in mind was that Maybe he would be given some money to buy coffee.

For a while, I believed that getting money for food and that cup of coffee was Robert's Maybe. I felt that in my efforts to coach him, I might have ignored what Robert really wanted from me because I thought he *should* want something different for his life. I thought that I had failed the realm of Maybe because I tried to create something for someone else when it did not truly resonate with what he wanted.

A few months later, I was fortunate to run into Robert on the street again. He had gotten pneumonia and just been released from the hospital. We talked for a while, and this time I tried just to listen to him and be with him. He told me he was working on getting housing for himself and his girlfriend and he was hoping that it would happen soon. He said his biggest concern was for his girlfriend's safety because she was sleeping on the street every night even when he was not around. He then said to me, "I so thank you and the doctors in the hospital for treating me like a human being. Some people walk by and spit on me. All these times when you stopped and talked to me, it gives me hope that people are good and Maybe my life can change for the better." I responded, "Robert, thank you. You give me hope that

Maybe my life can change for the better, too." As tears welled up in both of our eyes, we shook hands and said good-bye.

This conversation made me realize that Maybe what Robert had really needed from me was not a solution to his lack of employment or even lack of shelter. What he needed before he would commit to the possibility that his life could be different was to see that someone else cared.

I wish this story of Maybe had a happier ending, but Maybe isn't about endings. I stopped seeing Robert on the street for a time and began to hope that his housing had come through. One day, I was walking past the spot in the street where Robert used to panhandle and noticed a woman there. She was holding out a coffee cup and asking for money, too. For some reason, I decided to stop and, after putting a dollar in her cup, began to talk with her.

I learned that she was Robert's girlfriend. She told me, with tears in her eyes, that he had died a few months earlier. She also told me that, although she still asked for money in the street, she wasn't homeless anymore. The housing that Robert had applied for on their behalf had come through a week after his death and she now had a place to sleep every night. Every time I see her on the street, I think of how the gift of kindness gave Robert the strength to believe in Maybe.

With this belief, he created the possibility for his girlfriend to be safe at night long after he was gone.

TRY THIS

· · · · ·

A NEW SONG

In several religious and spiritual traditions, a mantra is a phrase that you can repeat to yourself over and over in order to calm the mind or evoke other states of mind or emotion. When you embrace a "Maybe" mantra, no matter how difficult your circumstances, a lot can transform in your life by the simple power of repetition.

Keep the following mantra close to you, an expanded version of the single word:

"Even though my life has changed, my possibilities are still infinite. Maybe I can still find my way."

Use this mantra or develop your own over time. Write it down on a piece of paper and keep it on your desk. Sometimes people even use objects to remind them of their Maybe mantra. They keep a little trinket on their desk or stone in their pocket always reminding them that Maybe is by their side.

Life can get busy and situations can overwhelm us. What

makes this magical elixir called Maybe so easy to digest is that it does not ask us to have all the answers for our success. It does not require us to identify the path that will solve our problems. It just asks us to be aware that, within the field of Maybe, possibilities change but new ones are always there for us to access. When we have no idea what to do or what choice to make, our "Maybe" mantra allows us to clear our minds and see over time all of the exciting and rich possibilities in our lives.

SEVEN

The Internal Maybe: Finding a New Strength

.....

Your Inner Dialogue Revised

> Our doubts are traitors and make us lose the good
> we oft might win, by fearing to attempt.
>
> **—WILLIAM SHAKESPEARE**

Over the years, I have shared the philosophy of Maybe with many people and seen great success. Often in these meetings with clients, the magic of Maybe immediately opens up so many new doors that my clients leave my office hopeful and excited about all the possibilities ahead in their lives. Sometimes, however, I find that after a few sessions, a client has not made any new changes, even though he or she originally loved the idea of Maybe. I have seen clients struggle to get the best business ideas off the ground or not pursue amazing job opportunities or careers. These clients often tell me that they left my office excited about their new possibilities, but when faced with their inner uncertainty about their decisions or capabilities, they were unable to move forward.

The continuous problems that some of my clients had in their lives led me to realize that the philosophy of Maybe can also be applied to overcome the uncertainty that so many of us have, not only about our stock portfolios or our career paths, but about ourselves.

A little self-doubt can be useful, acting as a soft whisper in our lives that prevents us from making rash decisions when contemplating a new venture or idea. However, at other times our doubt can get so amplified that it creates confusion and keeps us from making clear decisions. Too much self-doubt contributes to a cycle of never-ending internal questions, such as "Am I sure I can do this?," "What happens if I fail?," "What if my idea is foolish?," "How will other people judge me?" As this chatter crowds our minds, it robs us of the courage and confidence to embrace all that really *is* possible.

The good news is this: Just as our fears about what will happen externally in our lives are not absolutely certain, neither are our doubts about ourselves. Can we be absolutely certain that we cannot achieve what we want in our lives? Are we absolutely certain that what other people think about what we do with our lives is correct? Are we absolutely certain that there is no way that we can create opportunities we desire? Most of the time, the answer to all of these questions is "No, we can't be certain!"

Yet, even knowing our doubts are not certain, it can still be very difficult to maintain a new perspective. Eventually, doubts from the past creep back in, and the battle between our goals and our fears continues. Often our self-doubt finds a tremendous amount of evidence from our past as to why we are stuck and cannot pursue new avenues in our lives. Our friends and family may have given us advice years ago to take another path or we failed at something that was meaningful, leaving us doubtful that we are competent to achieve our goals. Other times, someone powerful in our lives told us that we were not able to achieve something we wanted for ourselves, and we still believe this to be true. Whatever the reasons for our self-doubt, it can become a barrier that disconnects us from the firm platform we need to stand on in order to begin our journey.

Still, Maybe is a powerful antidote for our self-doubt. The concept of Maybe does not ask us to find the root of our inner uncertainty. Maybe doesn't ask us to resolve all the obstacles in our past or work through the regrets of all those paths not taken. It also does not ask us to be certain of anything. Instead, Maybe takes us where we stand in the moment and gently asks us to investigate what is possible going forward. It allows us to take a peek at changing aspects of our lives without feeling overwhelmed with everything that needs to get done. Maybe is a small step forward on a path that we never believed was possible to follow. Maybe, just Maybe, after we take one step, we are able to take another small step after that.

As we investigate our new mind-set, we realize that Maybe what other people told us about our capabilities is not true, Maybe the path we desire is still possible, or Maybe we *can* contemplate making changes in our lives that will bring us more joy and abundance. Maybe is a little ray of hope casting doubt on the past, a mind-set that allows us to embrace everything we are and all that we can achieve. Maybe helps us find our determination to start thinking about the business we dreamed of starting years ago or the career we never pursued. We find the strength to ask ourselves if these are things we would like to do today or if there are other pursuits that now interest us more.

Maybe begins to dilute the power of our self-doubt because we have that instant realization that Maybe we can achieve our goals. Maybe confronts every one of our beliefs that we don't have what it takes to succeed because, in fact, Maybe we do. Maybe is a soft and gentle reminder bringing us fully present to this moment with a fresh new look at ourselves and all that is possible for our future.

Don't Leave the Keys in the Door

I met Barbara when she had just ended her personal and business relationship with her partner of many years. He bought her out of the business for $25,000, and the very next day, she opened her doors to her own business venture. Barbara designed and manufactured promotional items such as cosmetic bags and totes for large companies all over the world, but her dream was to design and sell her own line of handbags. So as time went on, Barbara and I worked on growing her promotions business and using the profits to start the handbag business.

Although the business encompassed a great deal of her time and work, Barbara didn't mind because she was living her passion. Over the years, Barbara borrowed a great deal of money to further fund her business and her credit line was maxed out. One day, Barbara had a meeting with her accountant, and he told her that a woman her age (she was in her fifties) should not have so much debt—she'd be better off liquidating the business now, paying off her debts, and selling her apartment. He advised her to put all of the remaining money in the bank for her retirement. His final words were, "Barbara, leave the keys in the door and get out."

Right after that meeting, Barbara called me in tears and total panic. She was in a state of despair, and when I arrived at her office the next day, the first thing we did was review her financial statements and business plan. We went over all the business opportunities that were available at the time and the ones that she wanted to create in the future. All the possibilities were there, as they always had been, but after hearing her accountant's gloomy scenario, Barbara could only see her self-doubt. We had worked together for more than eight years, and the word "bankruptcy" had never come up between us. It was as if Barbara had given up her dream and now owned the reality that her accountant had sold to her.

At this point in our meeting, I realized all of the budgets and financial statements in the world could not help Barbara in this moment. I began to gather together the many papers on the desk and put them aside. I looked straight at Barbara and asked, "What is your dream?"

Barbara glanced at me, paused, and then answered, "My dream is to run a successful handbag company."

I then asked Barbara, "How would you feel if you never gave the business more of a shot and bailed out right now?"

She hesitated for a moment and then said, "I would live a life of regret."

I quickly responded, "So whose reality is bankruptcy or liquidation? It is certainly not yours!" I then asked Barbara to create some Maybe statements that she could use when she began to doubt herself or her dream of growing her business. Barbara wrote some statements down and then looked up at me and smiled. "Maybe I can do this and everything is exactly as it should be. I don't have all the answers right now to pay off my credit line but Maybe that is okay. Maybe I should start listening to myself and not my accountant! Now that feels good," she responded joyfully.

Maybe gave Barbara the inner strength to see the possibility that her accountant was wrong about his advice and she was capable of continuing to grow her business. Since that time, Barbara has fired her accountant and worked diligently toward expanding her business. For years, she used Maybe on a daily basis to help her weather economic uncertainty, failed business relationships, production issues, and various other problems that faced her business. Barbara continued to sell her beautifully crafted leather handbags worldwide and eventually, with an increase in sales, was able to pay off the credit line that she took out in those tough times five years earlier. Recently Barbara told me that she is thinking of retiring in about five years, but not by liquidation or bankruptcy. Instead, she is considering the very real option of selling her company for millions of dollars and traveling around the world.

Fear of Failure

> I failed my way to success.
>
> **—THOMAS EDISON**

One of the most common issues my clients have when they want to start a new business, change their careers, or set new goals is a fear of failure. Some see failure as the end of the road for every endeavor and start to question their ability to avoid this fatal blow to their dreams. The uncertainty about their success makes them question their abilities to find all the answers before they begin or question their aptitude to deal with all the scenarios that can occur in this new terrain. Yet when I introduce the idea of Maybe for their inner uncertainty, my clients start to change their relationships with both the fear of failure and with failure itself. The results are overwhelming, and I hope the following examples will inspire you, too.

A young woman comes to the United States with no family, no money, and a dream to become a teacher. She works hard as a childcare provider for years and takes classes at night. Several times her credit card bills are so high she can barely make tuition payments, and sometimes there is little time to study and her grades suffer. After ten years of managing all the demands in her life, she graduates. Today, she is an elementary school teacher.

A young girl tries out for several musical plays over the years with no success. First, she does not even make the cast list, but eventually she is in several ensembles with little time on the stage. With some hard work and determination, she realizes she is a much better actress than singer and even quite funny. She finally gets a small speaking role in a school drama and eventually, a year later, one of the lead roles.

For many years a man works in the construction industry

Failure was just a stepping-stone for what was possible.

for various companies. Each job has its aggravation and challenges, and every time he takes a new job he is unable to successfully take a lead role at the company. He becomes overweight, feels sick from his stress, and has conflicts with each of his bosses. Finally, he takes some time off, regains his health, and successfully starts his own construction company.

My last example is this. An author gets rejected more than twenty times from various publishers but never gives up. She starts a blog and continues to work hard on spreading the message in her book, which she just knows will help so many people. After several years of growing her following and widening her platform, she gets a book deal with the largest publisher in the world. Can you guess who I'm talking about? Yes, me!

What did these four people have in common? They all used Maybe to quell their self-doubt and believe in their dreams. Failure was just a stepping-stone for what was possible, not an indication of what each of them was capable of achieving. Each of them at one time or another could be heard saying, "Maybe I can still find a way to make this happen," and eventually each of them did.

As long as we see the Maybe in our experiences, fear of failure falls away. We realize that the next moment will bring more possibilities to find the success we yearn for. In place of our fear of failure and self-doubt, there is an inner strength calling on us to take action in order to change our lives. Our lives become less about what we can't achieve or how many times we need to exhaust ourselves attempting to reach our goals. Instead, we learn from our setbacks and have the confidence to try again.

There's a paradox here, a little secret I'll share with you now. When we embrace Maybe, we become less concerned with failure and *more certain* about one key aspect of our lives. We gain more certainty about *who we are* and what we want for our lives. We rest within the hope that Maybe we have everything we need within us to create the life that we truly desire, even if there are stumbling blocks along the way.

The Singing Attorney

When I met Stacey, she was happily married, a mother of two, and a working attorney. Our daughters were friends at school, and this gave us the opportunity to spend a few afternoons together as our children played. One day when we were together, the radio was on and Stacey began to sing. I was so taken aback by the beauty of her voice that I said, "You have such a beautiful voice. Have you ever considered singing professionally?"

Stacey answered me with her eyes down. "I'm an attorney and, anyway, who would ever hire me?"

Without any hesitation, I challenged her. "That's not what I asked! Let me rephrase the question in another way. Would you like to sing professionally without taking anything else into consideration?"

She thought for a moment before she answered. "Of course I would! It was my lifelong dream, but I let it go a long time ago, and now with my husband, my kids, my work, it would be an impossible road to travel." As we talked more I learned that, as a little girl, Stacey dreamed of becoming both a singer and an attorney. Her parents felt that the chances of becoming a singer were so unlikely that she had to focus on one thing, and that was to become an attorney. Listening to her parents, Stacey became full of self-doubt. She put aside her dreams of singing and focused on her studies to become an attorney.

Now I asked, "Is singing still your dream?"

She nodded her head yes.

I continued my questioning. "If it is still your dream, would you ever consider that Maybe one day you could sing in public, like in a local bar or at an amateur night?"

She smiled and said, "Maybe one day I will sing in public."

About six months later, Stacey was at a karaoke bar and with the thought of Maybe, she decided to get up and sing. After she was finished, a woman approached and asked her if she would consider singing backup in her husband's band. She said she would consider it and then agreed to an audition. The next day Stacey frantically called me and told me she had made a big mistake in agreeing to the audition. I asked her, "Is this self-doubt coming from what your parents told you?"

She answered quickly. "No, you helped me get through that issue. I can't do this because I may be judged poorly by others, and I feel like I will pass out onstage."

I asked her again, "Is this your dream?"

"Without question, yes!" she said.

"Does it bring you joy to sing?" She said yes, and I continued, "Then go with your joy and passion. This is not about what your parents, the band, or anyone else thinks. This is about you walking into your own joy. Just do it from that inner place that's been yearning to sing. Go into that Maybe!"

"Wish me luck," she said, and hung up the phone.

She went for her audition and was accepted as a backup singer in a rock-and-roll band. She sang backup for a while, and then the lead singer left the band and they asked Stacey to be their new lead singer. Stacey recently performed her first two gigs as lead singer at the Bitter End, a famous venue in New York City. Now, whenever I meet Stacey, I see a face filled with contentment. Her parting words to me at our last encounter were, "I have a family, I work as an attorney, and I am lead singer in a band. I am living my dream!"

TRY THIS

. . . . .

BUILDING COURAGE

If you know what you want for your life but self-doubt has been holding you back, Maybe can help you build a platform of courage and resilience to achieve your goals.

First, write down one to five goals that you have not pursued because you feared you would fail or because you feared you would be unable to obtain your desired results.

Now, hold your list of doubts up against Maybe. Ask yourself: Are you absolutely certain that you are not capable of achieving these things? Most likely, the answer is no. Now create some Maybe statements that help you build courage: Maybe I can achieve my goals; Maybe more is possible than I thought; Maybe it is okay not to have all the answers right now; Maybe I can take one step today toward what I want to achieve; Maybe what other people have told me in the past about my capabilities is not true. Create more statements each day or find the one that best supports your new venture.

No matter how minute the possibilities of Maybe may seem, they will start to enlarge as you peel away your self-doubt. Don't worry about how small or large your achievements are, and don't worry if you stay in the internal dialogue of Maybe for a while before anything changes. As long as you are building your courage to be who you really are and act toward what you want, Maybe will support you.

EIGHT

Adopting Maybe as a Life Philosophy

. . . . .

A Shift of Perspective

I have seen many people fully embrace Maybe, quit their jobs, and immediately find a much better position. I have witnessed others fully embrace Maybe and free themselves from feeling stressed and restricted while still working in an old job, enabling them a few months later to find a new job they preferred. I have also worked with clients who have fully embraced Maybe and whose shift of perspective enabled them to transform a job they loathed into a happy and fulfilling career.

My point is that in reality, it is not about the job or the relationship or the house or anything else as much as it is about adopting Maybe as our way of thinking. When we do this, we see all of the possibilities that life offers and are able to shift perspective, let go of how we think things *should* be, and enter a place where we access all that *can* be.

The significance of embracing Maybe as our mind-set is that it is about changing ourselves from within, even when outer circumstances seem unchangeable or dire. If we believe that our lives are difficult because the economy is bad, for instance, Maybe very quickly provides an internal foundation from which we are able to explore different routes to new results. Maybe does not require us to judge old strategies and methods; instead it asks us to surrender to the newness of each experience. Maybe helps us to give up our story that things are bad or they can't get better and accept that life unfolds in many different ways.

Just because we can't see a way out or how to make things better in a given moment doesn't mean that we won't find our way. What's more, letting go of our certainty and embracing Maybe doesn't mean we throw all caution to the wind. Maybe is not about risking everything you have to make something happen. It is merely a way to figure out what we really want and how to be flexible and open to achieving these objectives. It is simply about shifting our perspective or belief system to one that does not leave us feeling trapped, lost, or victimized.

Paradoxically, when we are faced with our *most* difficult challenges, if we can restrain ourselves from grasping for certainty to cushion our fall, we experience the most freedom. In our greatest moments of uncertainty, Maybe can guide us through challenges and give us the foundation to benefit from the changes life inevitably brings.

The King and His Friend

By now, you realize that the philosophy of Maybe can have many different applications. My own journey into Maybe began with the Taoist story of the farmer and his horse. As you get ready to embark on your own path into Maybe, I offer you another of my favorite stories, one that may remind you to think "just Maybe" as you face the unexpected.

A king had a close friend who had the habit of remarking "Maybe this is good" about every occurrence in life, no matter what it was. One day, the king and his friend were out hunting. The king's friend loaded a gun and handed it to the king, but, alas, the friend had loaded it improperly, and when the king fired it, his thumb was blown off.

"Maybe this is good!" exclaimed his friend.

The horrified and bleeding king was furious. "How can you say 'maybe this is good'? This is obviously horrible!" he shouted. The king put his friend in jail.

About a year later, the king went hunting by himself. Cannibals captured him and took him to their village. They tied his hands, stacked some wood, set up a stake, and bound him to it. As they came near to set fire to the wood, they noticed that the king was missing a thumb. Being superstitious, they never ate anyone who was less than whole. They untied the king and sent him on his way.

Full of remorse, the king rushed to the prison to release his friend.

"You were right—it *was* good," the king said.

The king told his friend how the missing thumb had saved his life and added, "I feel so sad that I locked you in jail. That was such a bad thing to do."

"No! Maybe it's good!" responded his delighted friend.

"Oh, how could it be good, my friend? I did a terrible thing to you while I owe you my life."

"Well," his friend replied, "if I hadn't been in prison,

Maybe I would have been hunting with you and those canni-bals would have eaten *me*."

A New Journey

I hope this book inspires you to use Maybe as a tool to access all that is possible in your life. Say your Maybe mantras. Do a meditation or a visualization or journal with the Maybe Mind on a daily basis. Remind yourself of Maybe when you are engaging in simple tasks like walking to an appointment, speaking with a friend or family member, or completing a project at work, and create the habit of opening up to every experience as it unfolds. When something you haven't planned for occurs, try to shrug your shoulders and think Maybe. In this way, when you feel stuck or uneasy or start to believe that life has only one lane, Maybe will be close at hand to support you through the uncertainty of the situation, giving you hope and strength to find your way.

Eventually, as you experience the power of Maybe again and again, it will free you to explore the unknown with all its hope for a brighter future. Maybe is a beautiful path clear of the debris of worry and stress, an open sky, a universe of open doors that will allow you to make new creations and opportunities, allow you to experience the here and now with an open mind and a full heart.

As we embrace Maybe in our lives, there is hope, there is light, and within us grows the seed of everything that can be with all its glorious possibilities.

May you all enjoy your journey into the land of Maybe!

ACKNOWLEDGMENTS

I am deeply grateful to many people for their love and support over the years.

I would like to thank my father, Henry Naiztat, for laboring through my original version of the book and sharing his insights and wisdom. To my mother, Lorraine Naiztat, for her unwavering support through the years, which made it possible for me to find my own way in the world.

To my family, friends, and teachers who often have been a lifeline for Maybe. Joel and Susan Carmen, Diane Naiztat, Alexander Ham, Peter and Naomi Naiztat, Erica Naiztat, Shari and Dani Seiner, Allyson and Brett Kaufman, Debbie Naiztat, Mara, Alexandra, and Ian Kaye, Robin and Marc Miller, Michael Hiller, Mary Lynn Nicholas, Devorah Medwin, Alan Steinfeld, Kate Walbert, Lori Campbell, Michael Stefanakis, Laila DeGuzman, Sarah Bryden-Brown, Susan Fauls, Merrill Rudin, Libby Johnson, Joshua Rosenthal, Alexandra Max, John Phillipe Mathieu, Fiona Duff Kahn, Joel Kaye, Peter Fleissig, Marlene Litwin, Marie Benesh, Andrew Turetsky, Aida Turturro, Donna Wilkinson, Sat Hon, Hari Kaur, Olivier Bros, and Barbara Wosinski.

To Linda Chester, my literary agent, thank you for believing in Maybe in the early stages and having such a clear vision. Your direction and advice has been invaluable every step of the way.

ACKNOWLEDGMENTS

To Kyra Ryan, thank you for your friendship, genius editing skills, and ability to understand the idea of Maybe at its deepest levels.

To Marian Lizzi, the editor in chief of Perigee, I knew the minute I met you that *The Gift of Maybe* was in good hands and would reach many people with its powerful message. Thank you for your wonderful support. I also would like to thank Lisa Amoroso, the art director at Perigee, who designed the beautiful cover, and Tiffany Estreicher, who designed the interior pages. It has been an honor and a privilege to make Perigee the home for *The Gift of Maybe*.

To the three shining lights in my life, Mark, Morgan, and Amanda Carmen, whose love, patience, and support for Maybe made it possible.

Last, but not least, to everyone who reads this book. We might never meet in person but the infinite bond of Maybe will always connect us.

Allison Carmen was a stressed-out attorney working at a large law firm in Manhattan, searching for anything she could find to alleviate her emotional suffering. One day she heard an ancient parable that would change her life. In that one moment, she felt her heart open. She felt present, peaceful, and filled with hope—all centered around the idea of one simple word: Maybe. Maybe became the hope within uncertainty, offering her more than one way to approach all aspects of her life.

Today Allison is a business consultant, life coach, and spiritual adviser to people from all walks of life. Her blog, Facebook page, and YouTube videos have gained her an international following of people who are struggling with uncertainty and finding the hope they need to make important changes in their lives.

It is just one change of perspective, but Maybe it changes everything!

To learn more about the Philosophy of Maybe, visit
www.allisoncarmen.com